Two-Hour Christmas Crafts

200 Inspirational Decorating Ideas
to Celebrate the Season

Two-Hour Christmas Crafts

200 Inspirational Decorating Ideas
to Celebrate the Season

by Michele Thompson

Sterling Publishing Co., Inc. New York

A Sterling/Chapelle Book

To my mother.

Library of Congress Cataloging-in-Publication Data

Thompson, Michele.
    Two-hour Christmas crafts : 200 inspirational decorating ideas
to celebrate the season / by Michele Thompson.
        p.   cm.
    Includes index.
    ISBN 0-8069-9621-8
    1. Christmas decorations.   I. Title
TT900.C4T484   1999   99-14535
745.594'12--dc21   CIP

10   9   8   7   6   5   4   3   2   1

Published by Sterling Publishing Company, Inc.
387 Park Avenue South, New York, N.Y. 10016
© 1999 by Chapelle Limited
Distributed in Canada by Sterling Publishing
c/o Canadian Manda Group, One Atlantic Avenue, Suite 105
Toronto, Ontario, Canada M6K 3E7
Distributed in Great Britain and Europe by Cassell PLC
Wellington House, 125 Strand, London WC2R 0BB, England
Distributed in Australia by Capricorn Link (Australia) Pty Ltd.
P.O. Box 6651, Baulkham Hills, Business Centre, NSW 2153, Australia
Printed in Hong Kong

Sterling ISBN 0-8069-9621-8

For Chapelle Limited
Owner: Jo Packham
Editor: Ann Bear

Staff: Marie Barber,
Areta Bingham, Kass Burchett,
Rebecca Christensen, Dana Durney,
Holly Fuller, Marilyn Goff,
Holly Hollingsworth,
Susan Jorgensen, Barbara Milburn,
Linda Orton, Karmen Quinney,
Leslie Ridenour, Cindy Stoeckl

Photography: Kevin Dilley,
Photographer for Hazen Photography
Photo Stylist: Jo Packham

If you have any questions or
comments, please contact:
Chapelle, Ltd.
P.O. Box 9252
Ogden, UT 84409

(801) 621-2777
Fax (801) 621-2788
chapelle1@aol.com

Table of Contents

12

30

64

66

80

96

Copper-winged Finial Angel

Supplies

Acrylic paints (bronze; white)

Bead (large, wooden)

Crackle activator and medium

Finial (small, wooden)

Ornament hanger

Tooling copper (24-gauge)

Wire (24-gauge, copper)

Wood glue

Paint bead and finial bronze. Adhere bead to bottom of finial for angel head, making certain hole is on top. • Apply crackle activator, medium, and white paint to head and other desired areas of finial, following manufacturer's instructions. • Transfer Wings pattern on page 123 to tooling copper and cut out, using tin snips. • Score a design on wings, using a pointed tool, such as a nail. Punch holes in wings, as indicated on pattern, using a nail. • Thread wire through one hole from back to front. Wrap wire around finial. Thread wire back through second hole from front to back. • Twist ends together to secure, using needle-nose pliers. • Adhere hanger in hole for ornament.

Option: For French country-look, use wooden wings, light blue and white with acrylic paints, and antiquing medium.

Hardware Cloth Ornaments

Supplies (for two ornaments)

Hardware cloth

Hot-glue gun and glue sticks

Ornament hangers (2)

Spray paint (silver)

Tin motifs (2 rusty)

Paint one motif silver. Cut hardware cloth into desired size squares, using wire cutters. Adhere motifs to squares. Hang ornaments on tree with ornament hangers.

Rusty Tree Pin

Supplies

Hot-glue gun and glue sticks

Jewelry pin backing

Nail polish (clear)

Tin tree (rusty)

Wire (24-gauge, copper)

Paint back of tree with nail polish to prevent rust from staining clothing. Let dry. • Wrap wire around tree to decorate, using needle-nose pliers, as shown in photo. Shape top end of wire into star for tree topper. • Adhere pin backing to back of tree.

Rusty Ornament

Supplies

Beads (assorted)

Fabric (felt, scrap)

Hot-glue gun and glue sticks

Ornament hanger

Tin angel (rusty)

Wire (28-gauge, gold)

Punch a hole in each wing tip, using a nail. • Thread wire through one wing tip hole from back to front and string one bead, positioning it at center point of hanger. Twist wire to secure bead in place, using needle-nose pliers. • Thread wire through other wing tip hole from back to front. • Thread on beads for garland. Thread wire back through first hole from front to back. Twist ends together to secure. • Cut small circle from felt for back of head, using fabric scissors. • Curl several lengths of wire into spirals. Adhere spirals to felt, and felt to head.

Ornaments such as these are so simple, they can be made from any coloring book shape and out of any material. Shiny tin or copper, matte board, stiffened fabric, handmade paper, or thin sheets of painted wood are just some examples of the materials you can use.

Terra-cotta Card Holder

Supplies

Hot-glue gun and glue sticks

Plaster of paris

Terra-cotta pot (small, square)

Tin star

Wire (18-gauge)

Cut wire into desired number of 18" lengths, using wire cutters. • Secure lengths of wire together with masking tape at one end. Thread loose ends through pot hole from top to bottom until tape stops it. • Fill pot with plaster of paris, following manufacturer's instructions. Let dry. • Invert pot and curl ends of wires, using needle-nose pliers. • Adhere star to front of pot.

A terra-cotta pot can be designed to match any holiday decor. It could instantly become formal by gold-leafing, or Victorian by decoupaging flowered paper napkins on top.

Pinecone in Pot

Supplies

Ball ornaments (silver, small; 1 large, silver)

Hot-glue gun and glue sticks

Pinecone (giant)

Spray paint (silver)

Terra-cotta pot (medium)

Create geometric design on pot with masking tape. Paint pot silver. Let dry. Remove tape. • Adhere small ornaments to pinecone. Adhere large ornament to top of pinecone for tree topper. • Fill pot with weighty material, such as sand. • Place pinecone in pot.

Change from contemporary to country by painting snowmen, using a sponge brush, and adding snow to the tree with spray adhesive.

Bread Pan Candleholder

Supplies

Bread pan (metal)

Candles (5 square)

Glass rocks (3)

Sand

Super glue

Tin motifs (3 rusty)

Evenly space and adhere rocks to front of pan. Adhere rusty tin motifs to rocks. Fill pan half full with sand. Place candles in sand.

For a more traditional effect, paint the pan a high-gloss red and the stars shiny green.

Angel Ornament

Supplies

Acrylic paint (white)

Decorative button

Hot-glue gun and glue sticks

Terra-cotta pot (small)

Wire (18-gauge)

Paint pot white. Let dry. Lightly sand pot. • Cut a 15" length of wire, using wire cutters. Shape center of wire into circular head, using needle-nose pliers. • Twist ends of wire together and thread through hole in bottom of pot. Bend ends into "L" shape. • Cut two 8" lengths of wire for legs. Curl one end into a spiral and one end of each wire into a hook. Hook legs onto "L" inside pot. Invert pot. • Cut a 12" length of wire. Shape wire into halo and hang-er. Thread bottom of hanger through hole in pot and twist around head wire to secure. • Cut a 24" length of wire. Twist center of wire around base of head, then shape into wings. • Cut a 7" length of wire. Thread wire through wings and around pot. Twist in back to secure wings. • Adhere button to front of angel.

merry christmas

Mantel Cloth

Supplies

Fabric paint (gold)

Fabrics (lining; velvet)

Lettering (stencil)

Stencil brush

Tassels (gold)

Center and stencil words on velvet with fabric paint. Let dry. Sew lining to back of velvet, using a sewing machine. Hand-stitch one tassel to each point.

Coasters

Supplies

Cork sheet

Double-sided tape

Paper stars

Spray paints (gold; silver)

Cut round coasters from cork sheet, using utility knife. Paint coasters gold. Let dry. • Attach stars to center of coasters with double-sided tape. Paint coasters silver. Let dry. • Remove stars and tape to reveal gold stars beneath.

Wrought Iron Shelf

Supplies

Beads (assorted)

Nonpermanent glue

Ornaments (acorns)

Spray paint (silver-pine)

Wire (24-gauge, copper)

Wrought iron shelf

Paint shelf silver-pine. Let dry. • Cut an 8" length of wire for each ornament, using wire cutters. • Thread bead on wire. • Attach beaded wire to ornament hanger by threading wire through hanger and then back through bead hole. • Form loose end of wire into spiral, using needle-nose pliers. • Hang ornaments on shelf as shown in photo.

Nativity

Supplies

Acrylic paints (beige; white)

Craft glue

Decorative cords (assorted)

Glitter (gold; green; red)

Glitter spray (gold)

Rhinestones (assorted)

Scroll saw

Spray paint (gold)

Wire (paper-covered)

Wood (½"-thick pine)

Transfer Nativity patterns on pages 121–123 to wood. Cut nativity pieces from wood, using scroll saw. • Sand edges and remove dust. Paint wood pieces gold. Let dry. • Spray with gold glitter. Adhere rhinestones to crowns of wise men. • Apply a thin layer of glue on gift portion of wise men and sprinkle a different color of glitter on each. • Adhere decorative cord around heads of Joseph and shepherds. • Form staff from paper-covered wire and paint with gold spray paint. Adhere staff to one shepherd. • Paint baby Jesus with acrylic paints. Let dry. • Run thin lines of glue around baby Jesus as shown in photo. Sprinkle glue with gold glitter for straw.

Frosted Decanter

Supplies

Frosted decanter

Hot-glue gun and glue sticks

Wire (28-gauge, metallic red)

Cut wire to desired length. • Adhere end of wire to neck of decanter. Wrap wire around neck of decanter. • Curl end of wire into spiral, using needle-nose pliers, and let drape down the front of decanter.

Canister Box

Supplies

Craft glue

Drawer pull

Paper (textured)

Papier maché canister

Recycled beaded necklace

Cut paper to fit flush with top and bottom, with length slightly larger than circumference of canister, using craft scissors (lid is not covered). Adhere paper to canister, overlapping edges slightly. Screw drawer pull into center top of lid. Drape necklace around canister to embellish.

Rock Mosaic Card Holder

Supplies

Hot-glue gun and glue sticks

Plunger head (small)

Rocks (assorted, small)

Tile grout

Wire (18-gauge, uncovered floral)

Cut floral wire into 18" lengths, using wire cutters. Adhere wires into plunger where handle was. • Adhere small rocks to plunger head. Let dry. • Grout rocks, following manufacturer's instructions. Wipe grout from top of rocks, using a damp cloth or sponge. • Curl ends of wires into spirals, using needle-nose pliers. Slip cards into spirals.

Paper Angel Garland

Supplies

Craft glue

Papers (art; corrugated ribbon; textured)

Spray paints (gold; silver)

Fold textured paper in accordion pleat for desired number of angels and wide enough to fit Paper Angel pattern. • Transfer Paper Angel pattern on page 123 to folds and cut out. • Cut out face and feet from art paper and arms from textured paper, using craft scissors. Adhere to angel. • Paint a portion of corrugated paper silver. Cut hearts and stars from paper. Adhere to chest of angel. • Paint remaining corrugated paper ribbon gold. Cut into strips and curl around pencil. Adhere two strips to top of head for hair.

Brick Candleholders with Beeswax Candles

Supplies (for two candleholders)

Beeswax sheets (8)

Bricks (2)

Candlewicks (8)

Lay beeswax sheet on hard surface. Roll beeswax sheet around candlewick. The tighter it is rolled, the longer the candle will burn. Fill holes in brick with candles for a unique candleholder.

For a traditional look, paint bricks gold and use red beeswax sheets.

Lemon Leaf Kissing Ball

Supplies

Cold-glue gun and glue sticks

Dowel

Dried berries

Dried lemon leaves

Ribbon (narrow, red)

Spray paint (green)

Styrofoam ball

Tassel

Make a hole through center of ball, using dowel. Paint ball green. Let dry. • Adhere leaves and berries to ball. • Tie ribbon to tassel. Thread ribbon through ball from bottom to top. Use ribbon to hang.

Noel Candleholder

Supplies

Acrylic decorating paste

Cake decorating bag and #13 tip

Candle (votive)

Decoupage medium

Dishsoap

Nonpermanent marker

Paper (decorative tissue; white)

Vase (clear, glass)

Vinegar

Wash vase with dishsoap and vinegar water. Let dry. • Write "Noel" on white paper or print from computer. Slip paper to inside of glass with word facing out. Trace word on outside of glass with nonpermanent marker. Remove paper • Cut decorative paper to fit inside of vase, using craft scissors. • Decoupage paper to inside of vase, following manufacturer's instructions. Let dry. • Write word on vase with acrylic decorating paste, using decorating bag and #13 tip, following manufacturer's instructions. Place candle in vase.

Moss-covered Frame Wreath

Supplies

Dried berries

Evergreen sprigs (4)

Frame

Hot-glue gun and glue sticks

Moss

Pinecones (8–12 small)

Adhere moss on frame. Adhere evergreen sprigs, pinecones, and berries to corners of frame. Hang as wreath.

Frame wreaths can be made from frames of any shape or size, and covered with anything from greenery to tiny Christmas bells that will ring in the season.

White Tussy Mussy

Supplies

Evergreen sprig

Hot-glue gun and glue sticks

Paper (handmade)

Potpourri

Ribbon (decorative)

Shape paper into cone. Adhere together at seam. • Tip of cone is at bottom. Fold sides in at top. Make two vertical slits in front center 1" from top of cone and through to other side. Fill tussy mussy with potpourri. • Thread evergreen sprig through slits to close. Thread ribbon through top under evergreen sprig and tie into bow. Hang on doorknob or bedpost.

Paper tussy mussies are easily personalized. Create one for teenagers by making the cone from a sheet of popular music and attaching a gift certificate to a favorite concert.

Salt & Glitter Votive

Supplies

Candle (votive, white)

Candleholder (glass, square, votive)

Glitter (silver)

Salt

Skewer

Fill candleholder one-half to three-fourths full with salt. Cover top with layer of glitter. Poke glitter into salt, using skewer to create designs. Place candle in candleholder.

Simple projects have more impact when created in multiples. Make several votives filled with different colors of glitter and line your holiday mantle.

Artichoke Topiary

Supplies

Cup (silver, small)

Dried artichoke (small)

Floral foam

Spray paint (silver)

Paint artichoke silver. Let dry. Push floral foam into cup. Push artichoke stem into foam.

Almost anything can be substituted for an artichoke. Try an unusual item, such as a painted ornament or a fabric-wrapped ball.

Dried Flower Topiary

Supplies

Cold-glue gun and glue sticks

Cup (silver, small)

Dried flowers

Styrofoam ball

Run a thin line of glue around rim of cup and adhere styrofoam ball to cup. Adhere dried flowers to ball to cover the exposed surface.

In place of flowers, try old-fashioned sequins with bead centers.

Wire Mesh Bag

Supplies

Beads (assorted, seed)

Decorative button

Potpourri

Wire (beading)

Wire mesh

Cut mesh into rectangle, using wire cutters. Fold into envelope shape. • Cut envelope flap into triangle. Turn side seams and flap edges under ⅛" and finger-press tightly to secure edges together. • Cut wire to desired length for handle. Thread beads onto wire. Thread wire ends through mesh to secure handle to bag. • Attach button to flap with small piece of wire, using needle-nose pliers. Fill bag with potpourri.

Gold Mesh Box

Supplies

Beads (assorted)

Gold mesh box

Wire (beading)

Thread beads on wire. Wrap beaded wire around box and twist ends together, using needle-nose pliers. Secure beaded wire to box with additional wire.

Moss Star

Supplies

Craft glue

Decorative cord (gold)

Dried moss

Styrofoam star

Adhere moss to star. Wrap with gold cord.

Make a series of stars to decorate for the holidays. Experiment with dried flowers tied with silk ribbons, cloves wound with tiny gold threads, or adhere silver beads tied with copper wires.

Red Leaf Ball

Supplies

Cold-glue gun and glue sticks

Decorative straight pin (gold)

Eucalyptus leaves (long, red)

Ribbon (gold)

Styrofoam ball

Adhere eucalyptus leaves to ball in rows, beginning at top and working to bottom of ball. Tie ribbon into bow. Push straight pin through center of bow. Adhere pin and bow to ball by applying a small amount of glue on tip of pin and pushing pin into top of ball.

Wrap the styrofoam ball in Christmas fabric for a different look.

Painted Oriental Box

Supplies

Acrylic paints (black; gold; China red)

Box (wooden)

Lacquer

Paint box black. Let dry. Paint box with two coats of China red. Let dry. Paint oriental designs (examples can be found at local library) with gold paint. Let dry. Apply lacquer. Let dry.

An Art Nouveau stylized flower can replace the oriental art.

Wooden Star Ornament

Supplies

Acrylic paint (yellow)

Primitive star (wooden)

Tooling aluminum (36-gauge)

Wire (18-gauge)

Drill hole through one point on star, using a hand drill. • Paint star yellow. Let dry. Gently sand edges of star for distressed appearance. • Thread wire through hole and twist into decorative hanger, using needle-nose pliers. • Cut a primitive heart shape from aluminum, using tin snips. Nail heart to center of star.

Use as a gift tag on a gift for that special someone, or make a star ornament for each holiday guest. On the back side, personalize each one with a monogram, a word, or a short thought for the holiday season.

Snowman Clay Pin

Supplies

Acrylic paint (orange)

Beads (black, seed)

Jewelry pin backing

Oven-bake clay (blue; burgundy; white)

Wire (24-gauge, black)

Mold white clay into snowman. Mold blue and burgundy clays into striped scarf around snowman's neck. • Press beads into snowman for eyes, mouth, and buttons. Break off tip of toothpick and paint orange. Press toothpick into snowman's face for nose. • Cut wire into two small lengths, using wire cutters, and shape into arms. • Press arms into sides of snowman. Press pin backing into back of snowman. Bake snowman pin, following manufacturer's instructions.

Christmas Tree Clay Pin

Supplies

Beads (red, small)

Jewelry pin backing

Oven-bake clay (brown; green)

Mold green clay into triangle for tree. Press beads into tree for ornaments. • Mold brown clay into square for tree trunk. Press trunk into bottom of tree. • Press pin backing into back of tree. • Bake Christmas tree pin, following manufacturer's instructions.

Make some of your trees nontraditional. Try pink trees with tiny rose ornaments, copper trees with miniature silver balls, or brown trees with clove ornaments.

Round Pin Box

Supplies

Acrylic paint (dk. red)

Pin box (round, small, wooden)

Tooling aluminum (36-gauge)

Paint box dk. red. Let dry. Gently sand box for a distressed appearance. Cut a primitive star shape from aluminum, using tin snips. Nail star to center of box lid.

Almost everyone loves "little" boxes. Try putting a small holiday wish in each box, then fill a bowl with them by the front door and invite holiday guests to take one with them as they leave your home. It will be a pleasant surprise and a long-remembered gesture.

Napkin Stocking

Supplies

Beaded trim

Christmas stocking pattern

Napkins (2 large, linen)

Ribbon (grosgrain, wide)

Cut linen napkins, using Christmas stocking pattern and fabric scissors. Sew stocking, following pattern instructions, using sewing machine. • Hand-stitch beaded trim around bottom edge of ribbon, using a sewing needle. Fold ribbon in half lengthwise and sew over top of stocking for cuff. • Fold a small piece of ribbon into a loop and sew to inside of stocking for hanger.

Polka-dot Bowl

Supplies

Acrylic paint (yellow)

Metal bowl

Self-adhesive labels (colored, round)

Spray paint (red gloss)

Paint bowl yellow inside and out. Let dry. Randomly attach labels to outside of bowl. Paint outside of bowl red. Let dry. Remove labels to reveal polka dots. To clean bowl, wipe off with a soft cloth. Avoid using cleaners or soaking in water. Avoid use with food.

Line your party table with different colored polka-dot bowls.

Flower Apron

Supplies

Buttons (assorted)

Canvas apron with front pockets

Embroidery flosses (variegated brown; variegated green)

Embroidery needle

Fabric marker

Mark stem placement on front of apron, using fabric marker. Backstitch stems just inside pocket, using embroidery needle with six strands of desired floss. • Stitch buttons to stem ends, working thread from front of button, through, and back out to front, leaving long ends. Tie ends into bows.

If the cook in your home is the man of the house, in place of button flowers, pin team buttons at the end of "balloon-strings."

Triple Frame

Supplies

Acrylic paints (green; red; yellow)

Frames (3 wooden)

Wire (24-gauge, colored)

Using one color for each area and changing color for areas on each frame, paint sides, top, and border around opening of frames. Let dry. • Lay frames side by side. Drill two holes in appropriate sides of frames, using a hand drill, to connect them together. • Thread two strands of wire through holes to attach frames. Twist ends of wires together in back to secure, using needle-nose pliers.

Wire Votive Candleholder

Supplies

Beads (assorted)

Candle (votive)

Candleholder (votive, wire)

Wire (18-gauge)

Attach beads to candleholder with wire, using needle-nose pliers. Place candle in candleholder.

In place of beads, try attaching personal items for each family member—like a favorite old pin or badge that is no longer worn.

Chenille Christmas Stocking

Supplies

Christmas stocking pattern

Recycled chenille bedspread

Cut stocking, using Christmas stocking pattern and fabric scissors. Sew stocking, following pattern instructions, using sewing machine. Sew fringe of bedspread on top of stocking for cuff.

Oatmeal Box Luminary

Supplies

Candle (votive)

Copper foil (available at stained glass suppliers)

Hardware cloth

Oatmeal box

Rocks

Spray paint (copper)

Trace a Christmas tree or other motif onto oatmeal box. Carefully cut motif from oatmeal box, using utility knife. • Paint box copper, inside and out. Let dry. • Finish box top and motif edges with copper foil (foil is self-adhesive). • Cut hardware cloth, using wire cutters, large enough to set inside box and cover motif cutout, using wire cutters. • Set inside box. • Fill bottom of box with rocks. Place votive in center of rocks.

Etched "Glass" Shelf

Supplies

Drinking glasses (4)

Etching cream

Glass (¼" thick, cut to desired dimensions)

Etch desired design into drinking glasses with etching cream, following manufacturer's instructions. • To determine size of glass to be cut, space inverted glasses as desired. Measure end to end and add 4" for length. Width should be 4" larger than the bottom of the glasses. Set glass on etched drinking glasses.

Beaded Lampshade

Supplies

Acrylic paint (tan)

Beaded trim

Craft glue

Lampshade (paper)

Lightly sponge tan paint on lampshade. Let dry. Adhere beaded trim to inside bottom of lampshade.

Special Christmas lamps can be made by sponging the shade with paint and attaching tiny crystal snowflakes.

Wire Candle Topper

Supplies

Beads (assorted, seed)

Candle (votive)

Hardware cloth

Hot-glue gun and glue sticks

Small pot

Tin star

Wire (beading)

Shape hardware cloth into cone to fit over pot. • Tip of cone is top. Cut wire four times longer than bottom circumference of cone, using wire cutters. Thread beads onto wire. • Wrap wire around cone, securing ends to cone, using needle-nose pliers. • Adhere tin star to top of cone. • Place candle in pot, light candle, and cover with cone. Use caution and keep out of children's reach. Wire becomes hot when candle is lit.

Blue "Glass" Candleholder

Supplies

Candle (ball)

Glass (tall, tapered)

Glass frost medium (blue)

Ribbon (wire-edged)

Paint outside of glass with glass frost medium, following manufacturer's instructions. Let dry. Invert glass for candleholder. Tie bow around top portion of candleholder. Place candle on candleholder.

Blue Beaded Snowflake Ornament

Supplies

Beads (assorted, blue)

Flux (found at most hardware stores)

Soldering iron and solder

Wire (18-gauge)

Cut wire into four equal lengths, using wire cutters. Arrange wires in snowflake shape. Apply a small amount of flux to center and solder together. Thread beads onto wires as desired. Curl ends of wire, using needle-nose pliers.

Make several of these and hang them in your window.

Artichoke Candleholder

Supplies

Candle (pillar, tall)

Candle cup

Coaster (metal)

Fresh artichoke

Open center of artichoke. Place candle cup in center of artichoke. Place candle in cup. Let artichoke dry. Place artichoke on coaster.

Colorful holders that would smell wonderful through the holiday season can be made by replacing artichokes with oranges pierced with cloves. Hollow-out small sections of the oranges and push in candle cups.

Artichoke Candle Ring

Supplies

Ball ornaments
  (large, silver)

Berry spray (silver)

Candle (pillar)

Fresh artichokes
  (5–10 large)

Platter (large, silver)

Place candle in center of platter. Place artichokes around candle. Place ornaments and berry sprays as shown in photo.

Centerpieces such as this one make fabulous holiday hostess gifts that are inexpensive and easy to make. Buy inexpensive trays (even disposable aluminum cooking trays work) and ornaments from discount stores, or purchase them at the end of the season and save them for next year. Fill the tray with any fresh fruit or vegetable that will match the hostess' holiday decorations. Try being a little nontraditional— small red potatoes, a handmade candle, and distressed wooden ornaments would be the talk of her holiday guests.

Decorated Hand Towel

Supplies

Bells (gold, small)

Hand towel

Ribbon (4mm, silk;
  fringed, wide)

Velcro®

Cut fringed ribbon and three lengths of silk ribbon 2" longer than width of towel, using fabric scissors. • Sew silk ribbon to fringed ribbon in rows. • Tie silk ribbon bows on bells. Tack bows to fringed ribbon, using sewing needle. • Attach fringed ribbon around towel band with Velcro, wrapping and securing ends to back of towel. Remove ribbon before laundering.

Everything from hand towels to bath rugs are fun to decorate for the holidays. Any trim will work as long as it is attached in a manner that can be easily removed when the items need to be laundered.

Leaf & Berry Basket

Supplies

Fresh leaf and
  berry sprigs

Hot-glue gun and
  glue sticks

Twig basket

Arrange and adhere sprigs around rim of basket as shown in photo.

Ideas for decorating small holiday baskets are endless. For friends who are young at heart, try attaching small wooden toys in place of berries and leaves. Teenagers will like candy, grandmothers will like pieces of old jewelry, the men in your life will appreciate miniature sports paraphernalia. In addition, try beads, miniature ornaments, small silk flowers, and even tiny plastic fruit with real nuts!

Gold Frame

Supplies

Craft glue

Frame (wooden)

Glitter spray (gold)

Spray paint (gold)

Stars (gold, metal)

Wire (18-gauge, silver)

Paint frame gold. Let dry. Spray frame with glitter. Shape wire to form "Merry Christmas", using needle-nose pliers. Adhere "Merry Christmas" to frame. Adhere stars to frame as desired.

Glass Paperweights

Supplies (for two paperweights)

Glass glue (clear drying)

Permanent pen (metallic gold)

Sheet of glass (¼"-thick)

Snowflake sequin (gold, large)

Ask local glass company to cut sheet of glass into sixteen 2" squares and grind all edges smooth. Each paperweight requires eight glass squares. • Stack and adhere seven squares together for each paperweight, following manufacturer's instructions. Adhere sequin to top of one set of seven squares. Adhere eighth square over sequin. • Draw desired design or message on top of other set of seven squares, using permanent pen. Let dry. Adhere remaining square over top of design.

These truly are gifts that can be used by everyone. Personalize them with monograms or names, write thoughts, use cutouts or stickers.

Gift Box

Supplies

Fabric (gold, tulle)

Jingle bells (gold, large)

Papier maché box (large)

Ribbons (3 complementary colors and patterns, wide, wire-edged)

Spray paint (dk. green)

Paint box dk. green. Let dry. • Place gift inside. Cut tulle large enough to cover box with 6"–8" excess on each side for top of box, using fabric scissors. • Place box in center of tulle. Gather tulle up around box. Tie tulle together at center top of box with ribbons and bells. • Shape ribbons as desired.

Miniature Travel Trunk Box

Supplies (for one box)

Brass corners (4 small)

Decorative cord

Decoupage medium

Gift tag

Paper (assorted)

Papier maché box (small)

Cut paper to fit separately around box sides, box lid, and lid sides, using craft scissors. • Decoupage papers to box and lid. • Nail brass corners to box lid corners. • Cut two lengths of ribbon, twice the circumference of box. • Tie each ribbon around box and knot for straps of trunk. Center knots on side of box. Tie loose end of one ribbon to other ribbon at knot for handle of trunk. Repeat for opposite ribbon. • Tie gift tag to ribbon. Trim excess ribbon.

Rusty Star Box

Supplies

Cinnamon sticks

Cord (hemp)

Decoupage medium

Hot-glue gun and glue sticks

Paper (corrugated; handmade)

Papier maché box

Tin stars (1 large, rusty with
    prepunched holes;
    2 small, rusty)

Decoupage box with handmade paper, following manufacturer's instructions, overlapping edges slightly. Adhere cinnamon sticks in a tight row to box lid with hot glue. • Adhere a strip of corrugated paper around box. Wrap cord around box and through holes in large star and knot. • Adhere large star to box. Adhere small stars to ends of cord.

Make unique boxes for everyone. On some you may use embossed wrapping paper and hang a crystal star, or handmade paper with elegant tassels.

Decorative Trim Box

Supplies

Covered box (with clasp)

Decorative trims
    (3 complimentary)

Hot-glue gun and glue sticks

Adhere one decorative trim to box so edge fits just under lid. Adhere remaining decorative trims to lid.

Have the children make these for each of their friends. It is easy for them to glue on their favorite trims.

Handmade Paper Box

Supplies

Glue stick

Handmade paper (3 colors)

Papier maché box

Spray Adhesive

Adhere paper to box with spray adhesive, overlapping edges slightly. Adhere paper to lid with glue stick. Hand-tear contrasting paper into Christmas motif. Adhere to box with spray adhesive.

This is the perfect Christmas party project. Have each guest make their own box and then fill them with holiday cookies and candies.

Twig Star

Supplies

Raffia

Twigs (5 of equal length)

Tie ends of twigs together with raffia to form a star. Tie additional raffia on one tip of star for hanger.

Artichoke Pot

Supplies

Berry picks (gold)

Dried moss

Florist foam

Fresh artichokes (5–10 large)

Garland (sliver bead)

Gilded lemon leaves

Hot-glue gun and glue sticks

Ornaments (assorted)

Skewers (wooden)

Terra-cotta pot (large)

Tree branches

Wire (18-gauge)

Place foam in pot and push branches into foam. Fill empty space around branches with florist foam. • Adhere leaves to one end of skewers. Push skewers into foam to encircle branches with leaves. • Cut wire into appropriate lengths, using wire cutters. Wrap wire around artichoke stems. Push wires into foam to encircle leaves with artichokes. • Push gold berry picks between artichokes. Spread moss around top of pot to cover foam. Decorate tree with garland and ornaments as desired.

Holiday decorating can be so easy and fun that it is sometimes difficult to know which theme to choose and when to stop! These trees can be made and decorated in so many ways. For one, paint the pot blue, fill the pot with styrofoam balls painted with white snow-like paint, spray the tree branches with adhesive and sprinkle glitter snow on them, then hang tiny icicles and snow flakes from the branches. Another tree could be covered with tiny pieces of moss with miniature birds and bird's nests adhered to the branches. Keep the pot natural and fill with speckled wooden eggs.

Boxwood & Lemon Leaf Wreath

Supplies

Bells (4 rusty)

Boxwood branches

Dried lemon leaves

Grapevine wreath

Ribbon (silk)

Wire (18-gauge, green)

Arrange, alternating branches and leaves on wreath. • Cut 10" lengths of wire, using wire cutter. Secure branches and leaves by twisting wire around wreath, using needle-nose pliers. Cut loose ends of wire. • Attach a rusty bell on wire every quarter-turn of the wreath. • Tie ribbon to wreath.

Vary the look of the wreath by gold-leafing some of the lemon leaves; adhering synthetic snow to them with spray adhesive; sponge-painting them with glitter paint; or even lightly misting them with pastel spray paint.

Rusty Christmas Tree

Supplies

Tomato cage

Wire (16-gauge, rusty)

Invert tomato cage for tree. Form wire stars in squares and top of cage, using needle-nose pliers.

These trees are perfect for country decorating themes. Line them down the center of your holiday table and use only wooden serving bowls and natural wood chargers to carry out the theme.

Stenciled Bucket

Supplies

Acrylic paints (brown; green)

Dried moss

Fresh miniature pine tree (Alberta spruce)

Miniature lights

Ribbon (gold, wire-edged)

Pinecones (small)

Stencil brush

Stencil paper

Tin bucket (time worn)

Enlarge and transfer Pine Spray pattern on page 124 onto paper. • Cut stencil on a piece of glass or protected surface, using utility knife. Stencil pinecone and branch onto bucket with brown and green paints, using stencil brush. Let dry. • Place tree in bucket. Fill empty space around tree with newspaper. Fill top of bucket with dried moss. • Place pinecones around base of tree. Place lights on tree. Wrap ribbon around tree to adorn.

So many possibilities, so little time! These buckets can be decorated a hundred different ways with as many different holiday themes. For an oriental-themed Christmas, paint the bucket a high-gloss red and stencil oriental symbols on the front. For a Victorian-themed Christmas, spray the bucket white, using lace on the bucket as a stencil, and stencil roses as a border. For a contemporary-themed Christmas, paint the bucket chartreuse and stencil trees around in a variety of neon citrus colors. The only limits are your own imagination!

Grapevine Christmas Tree

Supplies

Grapevine garland

Grapevine star

Miniature lights

Tomato cage

Wire (18-gauge)

Invert tomato cage for tree. Wrap garland around tree, securing to cage with wire, using wire cutters. Wire star to top of tree. String lights on garland and star.

This tree is perfect to decorate the walkway to your front door. Simply make several trees, all of which look alike, or all of which are adorned with different color lights. Place them at intervals to light the way for your holiday guests.

Wire Basket

Supplies

Fresh-cut evergreens

Grapevine ornaments

Greenery (assorted Christmas)

Pinecones

Wire basket

Fill bottom of wire basket with pinecones. Place evergreens in basket. • Arrange greenery, such as holly, pepper berries, or bay leaves, as desired. • Place ornaments in basket.

Replace greenery and pinecones with seasonal decorations, such as moss and live or artificial plants. This basket is a great idea to decorate a porch or hearth.

Tin Star Bottle

Supplies

Bottle

Cork

Craft punch

Sheet metal (36-gauge aluminum

Super glue

Cut sheet metal ¼" larger than circumference of bottle and to desired height on bottle, using tin snips. • Punch out shapes from sheet metal with craft punch. Adhere punched sheet metal to bottle. • Trace top of cork onto sheet metal and cut out. Adhere to top of cork. • Cut ¼"-wide metal strip ¼" longer than circumference of cork. Adhere around cork flush with top. • Fill bottle with syrup, liquor, bath oil, etc.

These bottles are ideal bazaar items for extra Christmas cash. They can be wrapped with everything from tin to sheets of music, and each will be "perfect" for someone!

Tomato Cage Card Holder

Supplies

Clothespins (wooden)

Hot-glue gun and glue sticks

Metal bucket

Spray paint (green, red, yellow)

Tin tree

Tomato cage

Wire (18-gauge)

Invert tomato cage, bring ends together and secure with wire, using wire cutter and needle-nose pliers. • Paint bucket, half the clothespins, and tomato cage green. Paint remaining clothespins red and yellow. Let dry. • Pin tomato cage to bucket with clothespins. Pin remaining clothespins to tomato cage. • Adhere tin Christmas tree to bucket. • Use pins to display cards.

Hardware Cloth Luminary

Supplies

Candle (small, pillar)

Glass rocks

Hardware cloth

Wire (20-gauge)

Cut five equal size squares from hardware cloth, using wire cutters. • Form squares into open-ended cube and secure edges with wire, using needle-nose pliers. • Set candle in center of wire cube. Surround candle with glass rocks. • Use caution and keep out of children's reach. Wire may become hot when candle is lit.

Hardware cloth can be sprayed a variety of colors or treated with a variety of finishes. Make certain that whatever is used is heat safe.

Christmas Crackle Advent Tree

Supplies

Acrylic paint (gold, green, red)

Crackle activator and medium

Drawer pulls (25 wooden)

Hot-glue gun and glue sticks

Ornaments (25 small)

Wood (small square, large triangle)

Paint drawer pulls and triangle gold for base coat. Let dry. • Apply crackle medium, activator, and red paint to drawer pulls following manufacturer's instructions. Let dry. • Apply crackle medium, activator, and green paint to triangle following manufacturer's instructions. Let dry. • Paint wood square red. Let dry. • Adhere square to bottom of triangle. Adhere drawer pulls to triangle. • Hang one ornament on a drawer pull every day in December until Christmas.

Lemon Tree in Copper Bucket

Supplies

Bucket (small, galvanized)

Craft glue

Dried moss

Dried lemon leaves

Floral foam

Hot-glue gun and glue sticks

Preformed topiary

Ribbon (6"-wide, copper, mesh; copper, narrow)

Spray paint (copper)

Paint bucket copper. Let dry. • Cut mesh ribbon long enough to wrap around bucket, using craft scissors. Wrap mesh ribbon around bucket and adhere with hot glue. • Wrap medium copper ribbon around bucket and tie into a bow. Adhere medium bow with a dot of hot glue under bow and on each side. • Fill bucket with floral foam. Push preformed topiary into foam. • Adhere leaves from bottom of topiary to top with craft glue, overlapping leaves slightly and offsetting rows. • Adhere moss to topiary base on inside of bucket.

Button & String Box

Supplies

Box (fabric covered, round, with clasp)

Buttons (6–7)

Hot-glue gun and glue sticks

String (packing)

Wrap string in a spiral around box. Adhere button to string on each revolution to secure.

Rustic Christmas Lampshade

Supplies

Bells (rusty)

Tin tree (rusty)

Foam adhesive dot

Paper lampshade

Wire (28-gauge)

Thread bells on wire, twisting wire around each bell to secure. Make belled wire long enough to fit the bottom circumference of lampshade. • Attach to bottom of lampshade by twisting ends of bell wire together, using needle-nose pliers. • Attach tree to lampshade with foam adhesive dot.

The lampshade also can be covered with fabric or painted for a completely different effect.

Crackle Box

Supplies

Acrylic paint (gold; ocre; yellow)

Box (wooden)

Crackle activator and medium

Finials (4 wooden)

Glass rock

Hot-glue gun and glue sticks

Wood glue

Paint box yellow for base coat. Paint finials gold. Let dry. • Apply crackle activator, medium and ocre paint, following manufacturer's instructions. Let dry. • Adhere inverted finials on bottom of box with wood glue. • Adhere glass rock on box lid with hot glue.

Potted Christmas Candle

Supplies

Candles (pillar; votive)

Garland (Christmas bead)

Square flower pot

Place pillar candle in middle of pot, extending 3"–4" above rim of pot. Fill pot with bead garland. When candle burns down to level of pot, discontinue use and place same color votive on top of pillar candle.

Velvet Aroma Bag

Supplies

Aromatic herbs

Beaded trim

Fabric (red, velvet)

Rice

Rubber stamp (bold)

Cut two squares of velvet, using fabric scissors. Place rubber stamp on ironing board, rubber side up, and one velvet square on rubber stamp with fabric right side down. • Lightly mist wrong side of velvet with water, and press stamp image into velvet, using iron approximately 30 seconds, on a medium heat setting (with no steam). • Place velvet squares with right sides together. Place beaded trim inside squares of fabric with raw edges flush with edge of beaded trim. • Sew three sides of bag, including beaded edge. Turn right side out and fill bag with aromatic herbs and rice. Hand-stitch opening closed, using sewing needle.

Crackle Coaster

Supplies (for one coaster)

Acrylic paint (dk. brown; lime green)

Antiquing gel

Crackle activator and medium

Decoupage medium

Paper Christmas motif

Wooden tile

Paint tile brown. Let dry. • Apply green paint, activator and crackle medium to tile, following manufacturer's instructions. Let dry. Decoupage motif to top of tile, following manufacturer's instructions. • Brush on a thin coat of antiquing gel and wipe off excess. Let dry.

For more personal coasters, try decoupaging family holiday photographs in place of a Christmas motif.

Velvet Gift Box

Supplies

Fabric (red, velvet)

Fusible web

Hot-glue gun and glue sticks

Papier maché box

Ribbon (narrow, lt. green)

Adhere fabric to box with fusible web, following manufacturer's instructions. Cover velvet box with ribbon. Tie a bow with ribbon. Adhere bow to lid.

In place of velvet, use quilted cotton, burlap or fleece with coordinating ties.

Magnolia Leaf Wreath

Supplies

Cardboard circle

Hot-glue gun and glue sticks

Dried magnolia leaves (large)

Spray paint (silver)

Paint leaves silver. Cut a large 1"-wide ring for wreath base from cardboard, using utility knife (cardboard circle from a frozen pizza works great). Adhere leaves to ring.

If you want a wreath that is much more detailed, try painting a small winter scene on some of the leaves, or decoupaging a thin printed paper napkin over an odd number of leaves. Carefully stored, these wreaths can be used for many seasons to come. If one leaf is damaged it is easily replaced—keep extras!

Wreath Candleholder

Supplies

Candles (4 pillar)

Candle cups (4 wooden)

Florist foam

Fresh greenery

Hot-glue gun and glue sticks

Spray paint (silver)

Wreath ring (wooden)

Paint wooden candle cups silver. Adhere candle cups to wooden wreath ring. Adhere foam to wreath. Push fresh greenery into florist foam and set candles into candle cups.

When making this wreath for the holidays, it is easy to change the look from party to party by simply adding something different to the greenery. Try a variety of fruits, wooden toys, unused ornaments, a selection of nuts, small wrapped packages, or whatever!

Pot with Magnolia Leaf Rim

Supplies

Acrylic paint (burgundy; metallic silver, textured)

Hot-glue gun and glue sticks

Dried magnolia leaves (large)

Leafing adhesive

Leafing sheets (silver)

Paintbrush (#10 flat)

Sponge brush

Spray paint (silver)

Terra-cotta pot (large)

Paint leaves silver. Let dry. • Paint vein on leaves with burgundy paint, using #10 flat. Let dry. Paint pot with silver metallic textured paint, using sponge brush. Let dry. • Apply leafing adhesive to outside of pot, using sponge brush. Do not apply adhesive to rim of pot. Let dry. Touch leafing sheet to pot here and there as desired. Do not cover all the painted area. Adhere leaves around rim of pot with hot glue, overlapping as you go. • Fill pot as desired.

You can have this pot coordinate with a wreath that is made from the same materials.

Silver Vase

Supplies

Ornament

Recycled vase

Spray paint (silver)

Paint vase silver. Place ornament on top of vase for display.

This is a perfect way to display favorite or antique ornaments. The vase can be any size or shape, and painted whatever color looks best with the ornament you wish to display. It may even be displayed after the holidays.

Silver Chiffon-wrapped Pot

Supplies

Ball ornaments
  (2 red)

Decorative cord
  (silver-tasseled)

Fabric (chiffon)

Spray paints (gold,
  silver)

Terra-cotta pot
  (medium)

Paint pot silver. Let dry. Twist and tuck newspaper to fit around plant inside pot. • Remove newspaper and paint gold. Let dry, then place back in pot. Cut a circle from chiffon large enough to wrap up around pot, using fabric scissors. • Fold raw edges under ¼" and sew with satin stitch to finish edge, using sewing needle. • Wrap pot with chiffon. Tie cord over top of pot. Attach ornaments to cord.

When wrapping pots, they can be wrapped with any type of fabric. For a more country-look, try cutting circles from calico fabric with decorative-edged scissors and tying them with jute and wooden nut crackers.

Cranberry Bottle

Supplies

Bottle (glass,
  long-necked)

Candle (pillar or
  tapered)

Cranberries

Ribbon (green)

Fill bottle with cranberries and water. Place candle in top of bottle. Tie ribbon into bow around bottle neck.

A bottle such as this can be filled with a variety of different objects. Try small nuts and berries, marbles, little polished rocks, even beads, buttons, or broken pieces of jewelry.

Ribbon Wreath

Supplies

Frame (wire wreath)

Ribbon (4"–6" wide,
  wire-edged)

Lay ribbon on top of frame. Wrap sides of ribbon to back of frame and tack, using sewing needle. Tie ends into bow.

When making wreaths as easy as this one, you can make smaller ones in multiples and use them for wrapping next year's packages. Try wrapping some in fabric, some in strips of old lace, or some in a variety of ribbons that were discarded from this year's packages.

Pinecone Kissing Ball

Supplies

Cold-glue gun and
  glue sticks

Dowel

Floral pins (2)

Pinecones (small)

Ribbon (green, wide)

Styrofoam ball (large)

Make a hole through center of ball, using dowel. Thread ribbon through hole. • Knot ribbon on one end of ball, leaving a tail for tassel. Tie bow close to ball on opposite end, leaving a long tail for hanger. • Adhere pins into ball and bow (at knot) with a dot of glue on each pin point. • Cut off flat bottom portion of pinecones, using a fine-toothed hand saw. Adhere flat pieces of pinecone to ball, overlapping to cover ball.

A kissing ball can be made from any item or items that can be glued to the styrofoam. One alternative would be broken pieces of jewelry, another would be silk flowers and berries, yet another would be frosted Christmas greenery with miniature ornaments.

Ribbon-laced Lampshade

Supplies

Craft glue

Lampshade
(paper-paneled)

Ribbon (green, silk)

Gently remove paper panels from lampshade. • Punch holes down sides of panels at same intervals on each panel, using paper punch. • Adhere panels back on lampshade frame. • Beginning at top, lace ribbon through holes and tie into bow at bottom of lampshade.

Ribbon Topiary

Supplies

Craft glue

Dowel

Dried moss

Floral foam

Floral pins

Ribbon (green, wide)

Spray paint (silver)

Styrofoam cone

Terra-cotta pot
(medium)

Cut dowel to 12" length, using fine-toothed hand saw. Paint dowel silver. Let dry. • Pin ribbon at bottom of cone, using floral pins. Wrap ribbon around cone and pin at top. • Tie another piece of ribbon into bow and pin to top of tree. • Fill pot with floral foam. Push dowel into center of cone for tree trunk. Push trunk into floral foam. Adhere moss over foam.

Ribbon topiaries can make a dramatic statement in any decorating theme if they are created and displayed in multiples. Line them along the top of your Christmas mantle or down the center of your dining room table. Choose any ribbon in any color!

Ribbon Star

Supplies

Hot-glue gun and
glue sticks

Ribbon (½"-wide,
lt. green)

Wreath (wire)

Adhere one end of ribbon to wreath. • Wrap ribbon around entire wreath to cover. Adhere ribbon at overlapping point, then continuing wrapping ribbon across wreath to form a star. Adhere final point of star, leaving extra ribbon on end for hanging.

The same design with a totally different effect can be achieved by using thin copper wire in place of ribbon, or tiny beaded trim that glistens when the lights hit them.

Corded Ball Ornament

Supplies

Beads (assorted)

Cold-glue gun and glue
sticks

Cord (narrow)

Decorative trim (narrow)

Dowel

Styrofoam ball

Tassel

Wire (20-gauge)

Make a hole through center of ball, using dowel. Thread wire through hole. • Adhere end of cord to bottom of ball. Wrap cord around diameter of ball until ball is covered and adhere end to top of ball. Cut trim into strips to fit vertically around ball, using fabric scissors. • Pin trim strips to ball at top and bottom. Thread beads onto bottom end of wire. • Shape end of wire into hook, using needle-nose pliers. Attach tassel to hook. • Thread beads onto top of wire. Curl top of wire into spiral.

Christmas Hand Towel

Supplies

Decorative trim
  (dk. green)

Fabric (green,
  terry cloth)

Hand towel (red)

Cut Christmas motif, such as a tree, from green terry cloth, using fabric scissors. Sew to red hand towel with satin stitch, using sewing machine. Hand-stitch decorative trim to edge of hand towel.

To make a more elegant guest towel for holiday guests, appliqué a beaded medallion onto an antique linen towel.

Tassel Box

Supplies

Decorative cord

Hot-glue gun and
  glue sticks

Ornament (glass,
  miniature, red)

Paper (shiny)

Papier maché box

Ribbon (1½"-wide,
  red)

Spray adhesive

Tassel

Adhere paper to box with spray adhesive. Tie tassel to cord. • Punch a hole in each side of box, using paper punch. Push ends of cord in each hole and secure with a knot. Adhere ribbon around lid with hot glue. • Punch a hole in top of lid and push in inverted ornament. Adhere ornament on inside of box lid.

Clear Christmas Stocking

Supplies

Clear vinyl

Christmas stocking
  pattern

Snowflake sequins
  (3 large)

Upholstery thread (red)

Cut stocking from vinyl, using Christmas stocking pattern and craft scissors. • Cut three squares from vinyl for pockets and sew to one stocking pattern piece, using sewing machine and upholstery thread. • Sew stocking pattern pieces together. Place snowflake sequin into each pocket.

Big and little "kids", alike, love stockings you can see through! In place of snowflake medallions, put baseball cards in the pockets of the stocking for the man in your life, and wrap all of his stocking presents in baseball-themed paper or with tiny baseball ornaments tied to the bows.

Christmas Plaid Placemat

Supplies

Decorative trim
  (green)

Large dish towel
  (green/red/white plaid)

Cut dish towel in half, using fabric scissors. Turn unfinished edge under ¼" and iron. Sew in place, using sewing machine. Sew decorative trim to edges.

Organdy Christmas Stocking

Supplies

Fabric (organdy)

Christmas stocking pattern

Cut stocking from organdy, using Christmas stocking pattern and fabric scissors. Sew stocking, following pattern instructions, using sewing machine. Place a clean cloth over stocking to iron.

These stockings are so easy and inexpensive to make that they can be made for all of the guests invited to your annual Christmas cookie party. It is such a wonderful sight to see 20 or more stockings—each a different color—filled to the brim with homemade Christmas cookies. This is a very special treat indeed!

Beaded Star Tomato Cage

Supplies

Beads (gold, white)

Flux (available at most hardware stores)

Spray paint (silver)

Soldering iron and solder

Tomato cage

Wire (18-gauge)

Invert tomato cage for tree and paint silver. Let dry. • Bend wire ends of tomato cage together, using needle-nose pliers. • Cut wire into four long and four short lengths, using wire cutters. Bend wires in star shape. • Apply a small amount of flux to center and solder together. Thread beads onto wire star as desired. • Curl ends of wires. Secure star to top of tree with wire.

Wire Bowl Candleholder

Supplies

Artificial fruit (plastic)

Beads (clear seed)

Candle (large, pillar)

Floral clay

Sequins (silver; copper)

Straight pins (½")

Wire bowl

Place candle in center of bowl and secure with floral clay. Thread one bead and one sequin on each pin. Push pins in fruit, overlapping sequins to cover. Place fruit in bowl around candle.

These fruits are a throwback to the '50's, but they are more popular today than they were then. Try them again or for the first time!

Organza Curtain Card Holder

Supplies

Cards or photos

Curtain rod

Fabric (organza)

Cut fabric to dimensions of window plus 3" on top and side, using fabric scissors. • Turn all edges in ¼" and iron. Fold edges in 1" more and sew along pressed edges, using sewing machine. • Leave ends of top open for curtain rod. If desired, sew tabs to top of curtain to hang. Cut assorted card-sized squares from remaining fabric for pockets, adding ¼" to all sides for turning. • Turn top edge in ¼" twice and sew. Turn other three sides in ¼" and iron. Arrange pockets on curtain as desired and sew around bottom and sides. • Hang curtain on curtain rod. Place cards or photos in pockets.

Painted Plate

Supplies   Plate (clear, glass)

Enamel paints
  (green; red)

Paint red circles on underside of plate. Let dry.
Paint green over red circles on underside of
plate. Let dry. When washing, be certain to
hand-wash.

*This is the perfect project for a child's Christ-
mas party. Each can take theirs home.*

Tole-painted Vinegar Jar

Supplies   Glaze (sparkle)

Acrylic paints   Paintbrushes (#2 flat;
  (avocado; black;   worn #2 flat; #8 flat;
  lt. blue; brown; dk.   #0 liner)
  green; orange;
  red; white)   Sponge brush

Glass and tile medium   Vinegar jar

Apply glass and tile medium to jar, using
sponge brush. • Transfer Snowman Scene
pattern on page 126 to jar. • Paint tree trunk
brown, using #0 liner. Stipple trees avocado
then dk. green, using worn #2 flat. • Stipple
snowman and snow mounds white. • Shade
behind mounds and bottom of snowman lt.
blue, using # 8 flat. Stipple white over lt. blue
shading to soften, using worn #2 flat. • Paint
eyes and mouth black, and nose orange, using
#0 liner. Paint hat black; hat band and scarf
red, using #2 flat. • Dab white on tree for snow,
using #0 liner. Fly-speck jar white. Paint sparkle
glaze over snow mounds, using #8 flat. • Apply
one coat of glass and tile medium over paint,
using sponge brush, following manufacturer's
instructions. Wipe with a damp cloth to clean.

Snowman

Supplies   Hot-glue gun and
      glue sticks
Acrylic paint (black;
  orange; white)   Jingle bells

Fabric glue   Oven-bake clay

Fabrics (green print;   Polyester stuffing
  red print; muslin)
      Wire (28-gauge)

Transfer Snowman pattern on page 125 to
muslin fabric and cut out, using fabric scissors.
• Sew arm pieces together, using sewing
machine, leaving top open. Turn and stuff. Pin
arms inside body sides and sew. • Sew gathering stitch around bottom. Sew body to base.
Turn and stuff. Close top. • Paint body and
arms white. Form eyes, mouth, and carrot nose
with clay. • Bake, following manufacturer's
instructions. • Paint eyes and mouth black.
Paint nose orange. • Sew hat. Turn and stuff.
Turn edges of hat brim and cuffs in ¼". • Adhere
brim to hat and cuffs to arms with fabric glue. •
Adhere hands to front of body. Adhere features
on face with hot glue. Embellish with wire and
bells as shown in photo.

Colorful Card Holder

Supplies   Quilt batting (thin)

Cork bulletin board   Spray paint (gold)

Decorative cord (gold)   Thumbtacks (flat-
      headed, gold)
Fabric (red)

Paint bulletin board frame gold. Let dry. • Cut
batting the size of cork board, using fabric
scissors. Cut fabric 1" larger than batting on all
sides. Cover batting with fabric, folding excess
fabric to back of batting. Tack to board. • Tack
ribbons in pattern across board. Slip cards
through ribbons.

Flowers in Vase

Supplies

Liquid resin

Silk flowers

Vase (clear, glass)

Pour liquid resin in vase, following manufacturer's instructions, and let set for two hours. Arrange silk flowers in vase. Gently rearrange flowers as resin sets. Resin will harden completely in 24 hours.

Christmas Cookie Plate

Supplies

Permanent pen (metallic gold)

White plate

Decorate plate with a Christmas wish and motifs, using metallic gold, permanent pen.

Create a cherished family tradition by having a special plate for "Santa's" cookies.

Napkin Ring

Supplies

Beads (assorted)

Empty toilet paper core

Wire (18-gauge)

Wrap wire around toilet paper core, using needle-nose pliers. Remove core and discard. • Thread assorted beads onto wire. Secure center of wire coil by wrapping additional wire tightly around coiled wire to secure.

Glass-tiled Picture Frame

Supplies

Enamel paint (gold)

Frame (resin)

Mosaic tiles (clear, glass, small)

Super glue

Paint simple gold designs on small glass mosaic tiles, using a very fine paintbrush. Let dry. Adhere painted surface of tiles to frame.

This is another project that is perfect for children at Christmas time; or for friends who think they have no talent for creating.

Painted Lampshade

Supplies

Acrylic paint
(raw sienna)

Lampshade (fabric)

Permanent marker
(black)

Sponge brush
(1"-wide)

Stencil brush

Stencil cream
(green; red)

Stencil paper

Trace Holly pattern on page 126 to stencil paper, using a black permanent marker. • Cut design out of paper on a piece of glass or protected surface, using a utility knife. • Tape stencil in place to lampshade with masking tape. Stencil leaves green and berries red. Mix acrylic paint with water for a washy consistency. Apply paint to lampshade, using sponge brush, applying darker around stencil an on edges of lampshade. • Blot with paper towels if needed. Let dry.

Decorated Christmas Tree

Supplies

Acrylic paint (gold; red)

Christmas tree (table-
top size)

String (packaging)

Varnish

Watercolor paper
(300 lb., cold-
pressed)

Cut Christmas motifs from paper for ornaments, using craft scissors. Punch a hole in each ornament, using paper punch. • Paint half of the ornaments with three coats of gold paint. Repeat with red paint on remaining ornaments. Let dry, then varnish. • When varnish is dry to touch, bend edges of ornaments to give dimension. • Tie string through holes. Hang ornaments on tree.

These ornaments are perfect "gifts" for holiday guests. Simply make a bowl full of ornaments, and on the back print a name or a heart-felt Christmas wish.

Wood-burned Nativity

Supplies

Acrylic paint (black;
blue; brown; gold;
gray; dk. green;
lt. green; lt. peach;
purple; dk. red;
lt. red; tan; white)

Scroll saw

Wood (½"-thick pine)

Wood burning tool

Transfer Nativity patterns on pages 121–123 to wood. • Cut nativity pieces from wood, using scroll saw. Sand edges and remove dust. Paint wood pieces as desired. Let dry. • Outline clothing and details, using wood burning tool.

Poinsettias in Suitcases

**Supplies (for two
suitcases)**

Poinsettias

Suitcases
(2 assorted, small)

Place poinsettias in open suitcases. "Pack" suitcases with other Christmas items.

Poinsettias need not always be displayed in traditional vases. Try something unusual—colorful red boots, sterling silver ice buckets, or paint cans with a painted holiday wish.

Silver Trees

Supplies (for two trees)

Ball ornaments (silver, small)

Dowel

Finial (metal, silver)

Florist foam

Hardware cloth

Hot-glue gun and glue sticks

Papier maché cones (2 hallow)

Spray paint (silver)

Terra-cotta pot (small)

Tin pail (small)

Wire (18-gauge)

Paint pot and cones silver. • Wrap hardware cloth around cones. • Fill cones, pail, and pot with florist foam. Cut dowel into two lengths, using fine-toothed hand saw. Push dowels into cones for trunks. Push trunks into pot and pail. • Adhere finial on top of one tree. Secure one ornament on top of other tree with wire, using needle-nose pliers. Adhere ornaments around bottom of tree.

Urn with Poinsettia

Supplies

Antiquing medium

Decorative cord (tasseled)

Dried moss

Floral pick

Leafing adhesive

Leafing sheets (silver)

Poinsettia

Spray paint (silver)

Urn

Whitewash medium

Paint urn silver. Let dry. Apply silver leafing to urn with leafing adhesive, following manufacturer's instructions. • Apply whitewash medium to urn. Let dry. Apply antiquing medium to urn. Let dry. • Tie cording around urn. Tuck floral pick in knot of cording. • Place poinsettia in urn. Tuck newspaper around plant to fill space. Cover newspaper with moss.

Silver-jeweled Ornament

Supplies

Ball ornament (silver)

Craft glue

Rhinestones (clear)

Adhere rhinestones on ornament.

Depending on the color of the ornament and the colors of the rhinestones, these Christmas balls can add an entirely new sparkle.

Stacked Boxes

Supplies

Ball ornaments (silver, small)

Craft glue

Paper hat boxes (3 for stacking)

Ribbons (3 complementary colors and patterns)

Wire (28-gauge)

Adhere ribbons around boxes and lids. Stack boxes and tie together with ribbon. Thread ornaments onto wire. Twist wire around ribbon bow for embellishment.

Fleece Stocking

Supplies

Christmas stocking pattern

Embroidery floss (bright)

Embroidery needle

Fabric (fleece)

Cut fabric, using Christmas stocking pattern and fabric scissors (or cut pattern pieces from old ski vest or hat). • Sew stocking, following pattern instructions, using sewing machine. • Blanket-stitch edges of stocking, cuff, and hanger, using embroidery needle with brightly colored floss.

Painted Mosaic Bottle

Supplies

Acrylic paint (red)

Beads (1 round red; 2 rectangular green)

Bottle (clear, glass)

Cork

Glass paint (green, red, white)

Grout

Paintbrush (#1 round)

Super glue

Tiles (⅝"-square, glass, green)

Wire (19-gauge gold)

Adhere tiles to bottle, leaving ⅛" space between tiles. Grout tiles, following manufacturer's instructions. • Wipe excess grout from tiles, using a damp sponge. • Paint cork with red acrylic paint. Dot flowers on bottle with red glass paint, using tip of paintbrush handle. Dot leaves under flowers with green. Randomly dot flowers and bottle with white, using tip of tooth-pick. Let dry. • Cut 10" length of wire, using wire cutters. Thread red bead onto wire and twist to secure, using needle-nose pliers. Thread one green bead on each side of red bead. • Twist wire ends together to secure. Cut off excess wire if needed. • Push wire ends in cork.

Pinecone Tree

Supplies

Acrylic paint (yellow)

Acrylic snow

Cinnamon stick

Decorative container

Floral foam

Glue stick

Hot-glue gun and glue sticks

Pinecone (large)

Plastic snow

Wooden star (dimensional)

Apply a large amount of hot glue to bottom of pinecone. Let glue begin to set, then push cinnamon stick into glue for tree trunk. Hold in place until glue is completely set. Apply more glue to secure stick in place. • Press floral foam into container and push tree trunk into foam. • Cover foam with plastic snow. • Dab acrylic snow on pinecone, using glue stick. Set aside to dry. • Paint star yellow. Adhere star to top of pinecone.

Holly-bedecked Pudding Mold

Supplies

Hot-glue gun and glue sticks

Miniature bells

Pudding mold

Spray paint (green)

Tin holly leaves

Wire (18-gauge)

Paint wire and holly leaves green. Let dry. • If premade leaves are not available, they may be cut from tooling aluminum, using tin snips, then spray-painted. • Adhere leaves to wire. Adhere bells to base of leaves for berries. • Drill two holes directly opposite each other in rim of mold, using hand drill. Bend ends of wires into hooks, using needle-nose pliers. Hook wire onto mold for handle.

Ivory Lampshade

Supplies

Elastic (¼"-wide)

Fabric (silk)

Ribbon (wire-edged)

Cut fabric twice the circumference of widest portion of lampshade and 3" taller than lampshade, using fabric scissors. • Sew a 1" casing at top of fabric. • Cut elastic ½" longer than the circumference of smallest portion of lampshade. Sew elastic 1" from casing. Sew a row of stitching 1" below elastic. • Sew ¼" hem at bottom. Iron wrong side of silk below last row of stitching, using a low heat setting and ironing cloth. • Sew fabric into tube. Put on lampshade and tie with ribbon.

Placemat Pillowcase

Supplies

Decorative trim

Fabric (large motif print)

Fusible web

Pillow

Placemats (2 solid colored)

Velcro®

Cut motifs from printed fabric, using fabric scissors. Adhere to center of one placemat with fusible web, following manufacturer's instructions. • Frame motifs with decorative trim. Sew Velcro to wrong side of one end of each placemat, ¾" from edge, using sewing machine. • Sew placemats together on other three sides with a ¾" seam allowance. Place pillow in pillowcase.

This charming pillowcase may be put on an existing pillow and removed at the end of the season.

Buttoned Hand Towel

Supplies

Buttons (3)

Hand towel

Ornaments (3)

Hand-stitch buttons to band of towel, using sewing needle. Hang ornaments from buttons. Remove ornaments before laundering.

Vary the buttons and the ornaments to fit every room! Try small sports buttons with laminated tickets hanging down.

Ribbon-wrapped Pot

Supplies (for one pot)

Ribbon (decorative)

Terra-cotta pot (glazed with separate saucer)

When purchasing, make certain saucer fits on top of pot. Set inverted saucer on top of pot. Wrap with ribbon and tie in a bow as shown in photo.

Here is a unique idea for gift wrapping, and a great idea for the garden enthusiast. Give gifts of seeds or potpourri.

Christmas Splendor

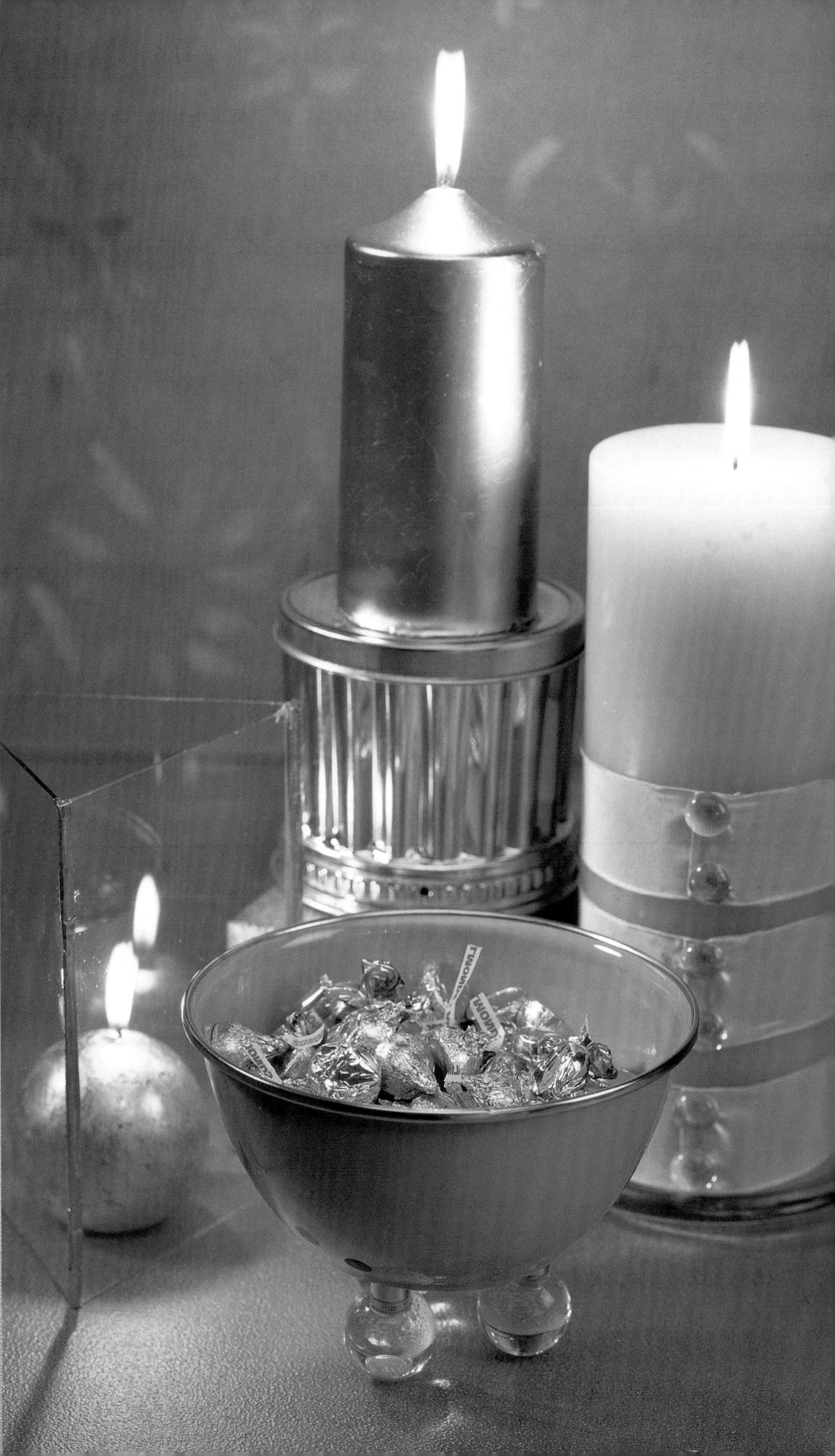

Treat Bowl

Supplies

Drawer pulls (3)

Super glue

Metal bowl

Adhere drawer pulls to bottom of bowl.

Tired of your serving dishes, but new ones are not in your budget? Buy inexpensive metal camping bowls, paint, and add "legs".

Ribbon-wrapped Candle

Supplies

Candle (large, pillar)

Glass rocks

Ribbon (wide)

Super glue

Cut three lengths of ribbon 1" larger than circumference of candle, using fabric scissors. • Wrap ribbons around candle, overlapping ends. Fold top overlap of ribbon under ½" to finish edge. • Tack ribbon edges together, using a sewing needle. Adhere rocks to ribbon seams.

Pudding Mold Candleholder

Supplies

Candle (large, pillar or tapered)

Pudding mold

Place candle on top of pudding mold for unique candleholder.

I love these! Instead of hiding them in the drawer, I made them into great candleholders to decorate my kitchen.

Glass Luminary

Supplies

Candle (ball, pillar, or tapered)

Copper foil (available at stained glass suppliers)

Glass glue (clear drying)

Glass rectangles (3)

Leafing adhesive

Leafing sheets (copper)

Apply copper leafing to candle with leafing adhesive, following manufacturer's instructions. • Stand glass rectangles together to form triangle and adhere with craft glue. • Finger-press copper foil along vertical edges of glass (foil is self-adhesive). • Place luminary over candle.

Try making these from pieces of colored glass. Stained glass makers in your area probably have small pieces left that they will sell you—what could be more colorful for the holidays?

Zen Frame Basic Assembly

Supplies for all frames

Acrylic paint

Frame (photo)

Matte board

River rocks (assorted, small)

Wash and dry rocks and set aside. Remove frame backing and glass. Cut matte board to fit back of frame, using craft scissors. Paint matte board to match frame. Staple board to back of frame. Continue assembly with one of the four options below.

Fountain of Wisdom

Additional supplies

Lettering (24-pt., rub-on)

Spray sealer

Follow instructions for Zen Frame Basic Assembly above. Position letters on rocks and rub on, following manufacturer's instructions. Apply sealer to rocks. Arrange rocks in frame as desired.

Christmas Zen

Additional supplies

Candle (medium, pillar)

Craft glue

Leafing adhesive

Leafing sheets (gold)

Sand

Follow instructions for Zen Frame Basic Assembly above. Apply gold leafing to candle and rocks with leafing adhesive, following manufacturer's instructions. Rub over candle and rocks with fingers to smooth. Adhere candle bottom to matte board. Fill frame with sand. Place rocks in sand.

Sand Garden

Additional supplies

Rake (small, wooden)

Sand

Follow instructions for Zen Frame Basic Assembly above. Fill frame with sand. Place rocks in sand. Rake desired design in sand.

Bonsai Christmas

Additional supplies

Bonsai tree

Sand

Follow instructions for Zen Frame Basic Assembly above. Fill frame with sand. Arrange tree and rocks in sand as desired.

Wire Mesh Tussy Mussy

Supplies

Decorative button

Flowers (artificial or fresh)

Hot-glue gun and glue sticks

Potpourri (optional)

Tooling aluminum (24-gauge)

Wire mesh

Shape mesh into cone. Adhere button to cone, securing mesh. • Shape aluminum into small cone. Adhere tip of aluminum cone. • Place mesh cone inside aluminum cone and adhere. • Fill tussy mussy with flowers as shown in photo or with potpourri.

These tussy mussies can be made in sizes that range from small ornament size to large table-top size. Use them throughout to fill the house with Christmas wonders.

Rose Tree

Supplies

Artificial Christmas tree (small)

Craft glue

Decorative container

Dried moss

Floral foam

Miniature light set

Picks (assorted berry; evergreen; floral)

Roses (silk)

Wire (24-gauge)

Fill container with floral foam. Push trunk of tree into foam. Adhere moss to foam. String lights on tree. Attach assorted picks and roses to tree branches with wire.

These trees can be made in any color and with any type of flower for the holidays. Use some-thing unusual—like yellow pansies, with yellow lights, berries, and bulbs.

Tole-painted Frame

Supplies

Acrylic paints (burgundy; med. green; lt. pink; off-white; lt. yellow)

Frame (resin)

Glass and tile medium

Paintbrushes (#4 flat; worn #4 flat; 10/0 scroller)

Sponge brush

Apply glass and tile medium to frame, using sponge brush. Let dry. Transfer Rose Corner pattern on page 120 to frame. • Double-load #4 flat paintbrush with burgundy on one side of the bristles and lt. pink on the other. Stroke on pallet to blend colors and soften. Stroke on the back portion of the rose's bowl. Stroke on front portion. Stroke on two petals on each side of the rose and one petal on the bottom. • Dot center of flower bowl with lt. yellow, using tip of paintbrush handle. • With a float of med. green, stroke on leaves and add the vein. • Load worn #4 flat paintbrush with off-white, stipple up and down to create filler flowers. • When paint is thoroughly dry, apply one coat of glass and tile medium over painting. To clean frame, wipe off with a soft cloth. Do not use cleaners on painted area or let soak in water.

Sheer Elegance Bottle Bag

Supplies

Bottle

Decorative cord

Fabric (organza)

Cut two equal-sized rectangular pieces of fabric, large enough to cover bottle, using fabric scissors. Sew fabric pieces on three sides. Hem raw edge. Place bottle in bag. Tie with decorative cord.

Lemon Leaf Swag

Supplies

Dried lemon leaves on branches

Fiber mesh

Ribbon (wide, wire-edged)

Wrap a bundle of leaves in mesh and tie with ribbon bow.

Any number of scented leaves can be tied with mesh and used for decorations during the holidays. Try small bundles of lavender for the tree, sprigs of sage for the kitchen, or mistletoe for the doorway.

Tortoise Vases

Supplies (for two vases)

Decorative vases (2 large)

Leafing adhesive

Leafing sheets (gold)

Ornaments (papier maché; glass, gold)

Apply gold leafing to papier maché ornament with leafing adhesive, following manufacturer's instructions. Place ornaments on top of vases for display.

This is also the perfect way to display antique or cherished ornaments that seem "lost" on the Christmas tree.

Copper Candleholders

Supplies (for two candleholders)

Candle (2 votive)

Candleholder (2 clear, votive)

Decorative ribbon

Decorative wax stamp

Hot-glue gun and glue sticks

Sealing wax

Spray paint (copper)

Paint candleholders copper on inside. Let dry. • Cut ribbon long enough to rap around candleholder and overlap ends slightly, using craft scissors. Wrap around candleholder and adhere ends. • Apply sealing wax to waxed paper. Stamp sealing wax. Remove stamped wax from paper and adhere to ribbon seam. • Place candle in holder.

Any inexpensive glass votive can be painted any color and wrapped with any type of thread to give as holiday gifts.

Wire Kissing Ball

Supplies

Mistletoe

Ribbons (gold mesh; silk)

Wire ball ornament

Slip mistletoe into ball. Tie ribbons into bows on top of ornament.

Kissing balls are so traditionally Christmas; but try something new and fill wire ornaments with any number of holiday decorations.

Glittery Gold Frame

Supplies

Decoupage medium

Frame (flat, wooden)

Glitter (gold)

Paper (Christmas tissue)

Spray paint (gold)

Paint frame gold. Mix gold glitter in decoupage medium. Decoupage tissue paper to frame, following manufacturer's instructions.

The possibilities for these frames are endless. Use any designed tissue and highlight with any color of glitter.

Star Frame

Supplies

Double-sided tape

Frame (flat, wooden)

Paper stars

Spray paints (gold; silver)

Paint frame gold. Let dry. Attach paper stars to frame with double-sided tape. Paint front of frame silver. Let dry. Remove paper stars and tape.

Make these frames to coordinate with a child's room. Use color combinations, such as red and blue, or brown and gold.

Silver Paper Frame

Supplies

Craft glue

Frame (flat, wooden)

Paper (textured)

Spray paint (silver)

Tin star

Cut paper to fit frame, using craft scissors. Adhere paper to frame. Paint frame silver. Let dry. Adhere star to frame.

Handmade papers of all kinds make beautiful frame finishes. Try one with flowers in the paper and adhere a porcelain rose; or use bark-looking paper and attach a twig or leaf.

Gold Beaded Frame

Supplies

Beads (gold glass, metal, round, small)

Frame (flat, wooden)

Hot-glue gun and glue sticks

Spray paint (gold)

Upholstery tacks (8)

Wire (24-gauge, gold)

Paint frame gold. Let dry. • Evenly position two tacks in each corner on back of frame and hammer in place. • Cut two pieces of wire to the length of frame plus 1", using wire cutters. Repeat for width of frame. • Thread beads on wires. Lay wires across frame, wrapping ends to back and around tacks to secure. Adhere each end of bead in place with a small amount of hot-glue.

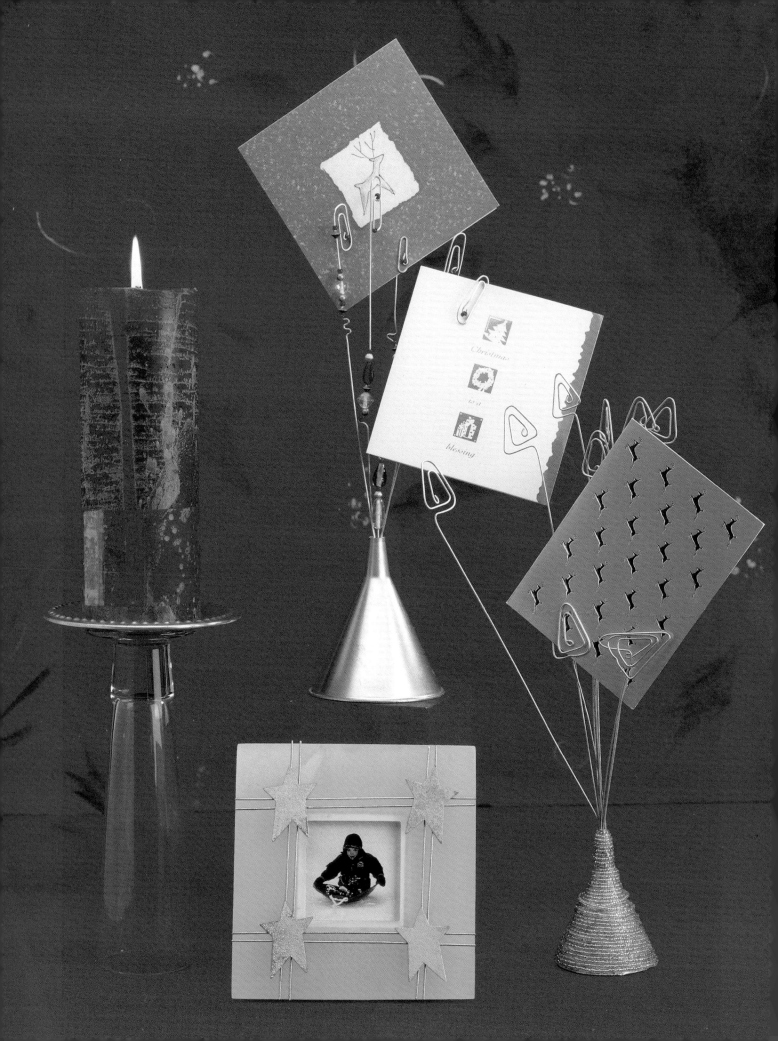

"Glass" Candleholder

Supplies

Candle (pillar)

Plate (silver)

Super glue

Tall glass

Adhere plate on inverted glass. Place candle on plate.

Silver Beaded Card Holder

Supplies

Beads (seed, silver)

Funnel (plastic, narrow-neck)

Hot-glue gun and glue sticks

Plaster of paris

Spray paint (silver)

Wire (18-gauge, beading)

Coat inside of funnel with petroleum jelly. • Cut wire into ten pieces of varying lengths, using wire cutters. Secure lengths of wire together on one end with masking tape. Push loose ends of wire from wide end through narrow end of funnel until tape stops it. • With free ends of wire down and wide mouth of funnel up, fill funnel with plaster of paris, following manu-facturer's instructions. Let dry. • Remove funnel and sand plaster smooth. Paint plaster silver. Let dry. • Bend free ends of wires into spiral triangles, using needle-nose pliers. • Adhere one end of beading wire to plaster. Thread beads on beading wire. Wrap beaded wire around plaster, covering plaster entirely. Wrap unbeaded end of beading wire around wire stems three times.

Red & Green Beaded Card Holder

Supplies

Beads (green; red)

Funnel (metal, narrow-neck)

Plaster of paris

Spray paint (silver)

Wire (18-gauge)

Paint funnel silver. Let dry. • Cut wire into five pieces of varying lengths, using wire cutters. Secure lengths of wire together on one end with masking tape. Push loose ends of wire from wide end through narrow end of funnel until tape stops it. • With free ends of wire down and wide mouth of funnel up, fill funnel with plaster of paris, following manufacturer's instructions. Let dry. • Thread beads on wires. Move beads to varying heights on wire. Bend wire at bottom and top of beads, using needle-nose pliers, to secure. • Bend top of wire into paper clip shape.

Metal Star Frame

Supplies

Frame (resin)

Hot-glue gun and glue sticks

Sheet metal (thin)

Wire (18-gauge)

Cut four pieces of wire each for length and width of frame, using wire cutters. • Arrange wires on frame as shown in photo and adhere. Cut stars from sheet metal, using tin snips. Adhere stars to wire intersections.

Try this with heart shapes, tree shapes, letters, numbers, or abstract cutouts.

Berry Topiary

Supplies

Berry picks

Craft glue

Dried moss

Small pot

Styrofoam ball

Run a thin line of craft glue around rim of pot and adhere styrofoam ball to pot. Adhere a thin layer of moss on styrofoam ball. Take apart berry picks and clip stems to ½" lengths in craft glue. Beginning at bottom, push stems into ball, as close to each other as possible.

Holly Coaster

Supplies

Acrylic paints (black; metallic gold; dk. green; lt. green; red; rose; white; yellow)

Fabric (canvas or sign cloth)

Paintbrushes (#8 flat; #12 flat; 10/0 scroller)

Transfer Holly pattern on page 126 to cloth and cut out. • Paint leaves lt. green and berries red, using #8 flat, until opaque for base. • Shade leaves and down one side of vein dk. green, using #12 flat. Highlight other side of leaf and vein with lt. green plus white. • Randomly apply thin washes of red, then yellow on leaves, using #8 flat to tint. • Shade berries with red plus black, using #12 flat. Highlight berries with rose. • Add metallic gold highlight strokes on berries, using scroller, as shown in photo.

Red & Green Beaded Snowflake Ornament

Supplies

Beads (assorted)

Flux (found at most hardware stores)

Soldering iron and solder

Wire (18-gauge)

Cut wire into four equal lengths, using wire cutters. Arrange wires in snowflake shape. Apply a small amount of flux to center and solder together. Thread beads onto wires as desired. Curl ends of wire, using needle-nose pliers.

Make each ornament with different beads—silver, stone, etc.

Rock-embellished Cake Plate

Supplies

Glass rocks

Matching glass bowl and plate

Super glue

Invert bowl and adhere plate to bottom of bowl. Adhere rocks around rim of plate to embellish.

This is a great idea—plates can be decorated in any motif!

Aroma Bag

Supplies (for one bag) Potpourri

Beads (assorted, seed) Ribbon (organdy,
contrasting color)
Fabric (organdy)

Cut a rectangle from fabric, using fabric scissors. • Cut two lengths of ribbon to fit width of fabric. Fold ribbons in half lengthwise over raw edges at top of fabric width and sew, using a sewing machine. • With right sides together, sew sides to form bag. Turn bag right side out. • Hand-stitch beads to front of bag to embellish, using sewing needle. Fill with potpourri. Tie bag closed with ribbon.

Option: For bag with handle and rose, cut desired length of ribbon for handle. Fork-cut ends as shown in Diagram A.

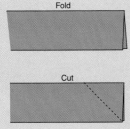
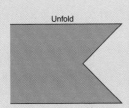

Diagram A

Tie knot 4" from each end. Tack knots to bag for handle. Close bag with rubber band. Tie ribbon around rubber band. Make ribbon rose as shown in Diagram B and tack on, using sewing needle.

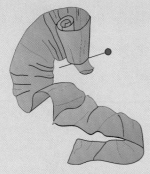

Diagram B

Decoupage Plate

Supplies

Decoupage medium

Fabric (abaca, gold)

Paper (Christmas tissue)

Plate (clear, glass)

Cut fabric to fit flat portion of plate bottom, using fabric scissors. Cut tissue paper in desired shapes to fit around rim of plate, using craft scissors. Decoupage tissue shapes on underside of rim, following manufacturer's instructions. Center and decoupage fabric to plate bottom.

Gold-topped Decanter

Supplies (for 1 decanter)

Decorative glass decanter

Leafing adhesive

Leafing sheets (gold)

Apply gold leafing to top of decanter and stopper with leafing adhesive, following manufacturer's instructions.

Glass Ornament Display

Supplies

Glass rocks

Ornament

Tassel

Vase (glass cylinder)

Fill bottom portion of vase with rocks. Tie tassel on top of ornament. Place inverted ornament on top of vase for display.

JOY

Terra-cotta Candleholder

Supplies

Acrylic paint (white)
Candle (votive)
Craft glue
Floral clay
Ribbon (velvet)
Sand
Sealing wax
Spray paint (silver)
Terra-cotta pot (small)

Paint inside of pot silver. Paint outside of pot white. Let dry. Gently sand outside of pot. • Adhere ribbon around rim of pot. Apply sealing wax to waxed paper. Stamp sealing wax. Remove stamped wax from paper and adhere to ribbon seam. • Seal drainage hole in bottom of pot with floral clay. Fill pot ¾ full with sand. Place candle in sand.

Candles like these can be as diverse as your friends—and just as much fun! Make some black and brown with animal print ribbons; brightly colored ones with polka-dot ribbons; or white and gold with lace ribbons.

Joy Frame

Supplies

Frame (flat, resin)
Lettering (stickers)

Personalize frame as desired with lettering.

It is fascinating how one word can make something so small mean so much. Try a name, a date, a word that has more than one meaning, or a series of words that goes around the frame. Display a photo of a special time with a friend.

Gold Beaded Snowflake Ornament

Supplies

Beads (assorted)
Flux (found at most hardware stores)
Soldering iron and solder
Wire (18-gauge)

Cut wire into four equal lengths, using wire cutters. Arrange wires in snowflake shape. • Apply a small amount of flux to center and solder together. • Thread beads onto wires as desired. Curl ends of wire, using needle-nose pliers.

Velvet Sachet Eye Pillow

Supplies

Aromatic herbs (chamomile; lavender)
Eyelet trim
Fabric (velvet)
Rice

Cut a rectangle from fabric, using fabric scissors. Fold fabric in half, with right sides together, and sew along two sides, using sewing machine. • Turn right side out. Fill with rice and aromatic herbs. Hand-stitch opening closed, using a sewing needle. • Cut trim to fit around short ends of pillow. Sew trim to pillow.

Scents have been proven to affect our moods. To unwind from a stressful day of holiday shopping, try lavender, rosemary, or clove in this luxurious and festive pillow. Place it over your eyes, sit back, and relax. To warm, place in microwave for 30 seconds. To cool, place in freezer.

Cross-stitch Kitchen Towel

Supplies

Acrylic paint (lt. yellow)

Beads (red, seed)

Button (small, wooden star)

Embroidery floss (variegated green; variegated rust)

Embroidery needle

Kitchen towel (with textured squares)

Paint button lt. yellow. Let dry. • Cross-stitch over textured squares of towel in a triangular Christmas tree pattern, skipping over every other row, using embroidery needle with six strands of floss. • Stitch a seed bead in center of each cross stitch on tree. Stitch button to top of tree.

These towels remind me of my grandmother. She would make us each one to match our kitchen, and give them with spices for our own holiday baking.

Wish List Clipboard

Supplies

Chain link

Clipboard

Copper foil (available at stained glass suppliers)

Copper tooling (36-gauge)

Enamel spray paints (copper; dk. green)

Wire (24-gauge, copper)

Paint clipboard dk. green and chain link copper. Finger-press copper foil around edge of clipboard. • Attach pen or pencil to chain link with wire. Attach chain link to back of clip. • Cut stars from copper tooling, using tin snips. Poke holes in stars for hanging, using nail. Wrap wire around top of clip and dangle stars from ends of wire.

Hang this cheery clipboard outside the front door for missed visitors to leave messages; or in the kitchen for children to fill out for Santa.

Dishcloth Pillow

Supplies

Dishclothes (2)

Grommets (4) and grommet tool

Pillow (small)

Ribbon (1½"-wide, red)

Place one dishcloth over each side of pillow. Pinch dishclothes together at center sides and attach grommets, using grommet tool. Thread ribbon through grommets and tie into knot or bow.

I love this idea because the same gift can look as different as each of my friends' kitchens. It is so fun to pick out the dishcloth for each.

Hurricane Lamp

Supplies

Ball ornaments (3)

Candle (pillar, tall)

Fabric glue

Greenery sprigs (3 assorted Christmas)

Hurricane lamp

Ribbon (red plaid)

Wire (24-gauge)

Wind ribbon around ends of sprigs and adhere end to secure. Tie a separate piece of ribbon around lamp, then tie another knot to attach sprigs. Tie ribbon ends into bow. • Attach ornaments to sprigs with wire. Tie another piece of ribbon into bow and attach to first bow with wire.

Velvet Cone

Supplies

Bead (glass)

Decorative trims

Dried flowers

Fabric (velvet)

Fabric glue

Styrofoam cone

Tassel (small)

Wrap fabric around cone and adhere. • Tip of cone is bottom. Adhere trims around top of cone. • Cut a piece of trim for hanger, using fabric scissors. • Adhere ends to inside of cone. • Thread end of tassel through glass bead and tack to bottom of cone, using sewing needle. • Fill cone with dried flowers.

Each year I make these cones to match our Christmas stockings. Some years they are playful, this year elegant, next year they will be very trendy—whatever suits me!

Burgundy Lampshade

Supplies

Cord (tasseled)

Fabric glue

Lampshade (small)

Ribbons (pleated, wide; 1½"-wide)

Choose a ribbon that is 1" wider than height of lampshade. Cut ribbons to the circumference of top of lampshade, using fabric scissors. • Sew ends of wider ribbon together, forming a tube, using sewing machine. Slip tube on lampshade, allowing ½" excess to fold naturally to inside top and bottom of lampshade. • Adhere 1½"-wide to top edge of wide ribbon with right side up, allowing 1½"-wide ribbon fold to inside of lampshade. Clip narrow ribbon to accommodate lampshade mechanism. Let dry. • Tie cord around lampshade.

Velvet Stocking

Supplies

Christmas stocking pattern

Cord (tasseled)

Fabrics (velvet, 2 complementary colors)

Cut one fabric, using Christmas stocking pattern and fabric scissors. Sew stocking, using sewing machine. Sew a cuff to stocking, using second fabric. • Tack tasseled cord inside top of stocking for hanger, using sewing needle.

Velvet stockings are so beautiful that I make new ones each year—depending on my decorating theme. One year I rubber-stamped on them; one year I beaded them; one year I painted on them; this year I left them plain.

Green Brocade Bag

Supplies

Fabric (brocade)

Fresh evergreen sprig

Potpourri

Ribbon (brown, silk)

Cut fabric into rectangle, using fabric scissors. • Fold fabric in half with right sides together. Sew one side seam. Turn down top of bag and sew to finish raw edge. Sew other side seam. Turn bag right side out. • Fill bag with potpourri, candy, or other favorite gift. Tie ribbon around bag to close. Tuck an evergreen sprig into ribbon knot.

I make several of these for the holidays and fill them with anything from candy to potpourri. I keep them in a bowl by the front door and give them to anyone who might come to visit. Each bag is different, so my guests can choose.

Golden Glitter Tree

Supplies

Craft glue

Finial (small, wooden)

Glitter spray (gold)

Gold glitter-tipped
  twig tree

Metal pail

Ribbon (gold,
  wire-edged)

Spray paint (gold)

Terra-cotta pot (small)

Paint clay pot, finial, and pail gold. Let dry. Spray each with glitter. • Fill bottom of pail with weighty material, such as sand, then stuff with newspaper. Set tree in pail. • Cut ribbon four times longer than bottom circumference of tree, using craft scissors. • Wrap ribbon around tree, and adhere ribbon ends to tree. • Adhere finial to bottom of clay pot. Invert clay pot and place as tree topper.

These look very different if the color is changed. My children's favorites were the ones done in all red or green.

Satin Tassel Pillow

Supplies

Decorative button

Fabric (satin)

Pillow

Tassel

Cut fabric 2½ times the height of pillow and the width of pillow plus 2", using fabric scissors. • With right sides together, fold fabric to the height of the pillow, allowing extra fabric at top for flap. Fabric should resemble an envelope. • Sew side seams, using sewing machine. Turn right side out and place pillow in pillowcase. • Fold corners of flap inside, making a V-shape, and tack closed with button, using sewing needle. • Hang tassel from button.

Pillows may be covered for the holidays and easily uncovered for everyday use. Diversify the fabrics for other holidays throughout the year.

Frosted Bottle

Supplies

Fabric paint
  writer (gold)

Frosted bottle

Permanent pen
  (metallic gold)

Rhinestones

Draw spiral designs on bottle, using permanent pen. Dab centers of spirals, using fabric paint writer. Press rhinestone into dab of wet paint. Let dry.

Note: A clear bottle may be frosted by applying glass frost medium to bottle, following manufacturer's instructions.

Gold-leafed Platter

Supplies

Acrylic paints
  (metallic gold;
  purple)

Leafing adhesive

Leafing sheets (gold)

Spray varnish

Platter (wooden)

Paint entire platter metallic gold. Let dry. • Apply gold leafing to rim of platter with leafing adhesive, following manufacturer's instructions. Crumble one sheet of gold leafing and apply to center of platter with leafing adhesive until desired amount of leafing is applied. • Paint a purple swirl in center of platter. Apply varnish to completed platter. • To clean, wipe with a damp cloth. Do not immerse in water or use soap.

Joy Candle

Supplies

Ball ornaments (silver, small)

Candle (large, pillar)

Wire (18-gauge; 28-gauge)

Cut length of 28-gauge wire to 2" larger than circumference of candle, using wire cutters. • Thread ornaments onto wire. • Wrap wire around candle for ring, twisting ends together to secure, using needle-nose pliers. • Shape 18-gauge wire into desired letters. • To attach letters to candle, cut ½" lengths of 28-gauge wire and wrap around sturdy section of letters. • Gently push wire ends into candle.

Bath Crystals Jar

Supplies

Bath crystals

Beads (assorted)

Cork (round)

Decorative bottle

Spray paint (purple; silver)

Super glue

Tin star

Wire (18-gauge)

Fill bottle with bath crystals. Paint cork purple and star silver. Let dry. Curl one end of wire into spiral, using needle-nose pliers. Thread beads onto wire. Push end of wire into cork. Place cork in bottle. Adhere tin star to front of bottle.

These gifts are beautiful, yet practical. My friends love to pamper themselves, and every year I give them one of these. I choose a different theme each year—every jar decorated a little differently, but the same. They each have their own collections!

Round Metal Box

Supplies

Box (galvanized metal)

Drawer pull (decorative)

Recycled necklace

Drill hole in center of box lid, using a hand drill. Screw drawer pull into hole. Drape necklace over box lid for decorative touch.

Use these to give tiny Christmas cakes to neighbors each year.

Silver Ball Wreath

Supplies

Ball ornaments (silver)

Berry picks (silver)

Hot-glue gun and glue sticks

Wire (20-gauge)

Wreath (artificial or fresh pine)

Cut 8" length of wire for each ornament, using wire cutters. Attach ornaments onto wreath with wire. Adhere berry picks to wreath.

Simple, yet elegant. I give one of these to each grown family member for their homes each year—always in a different color. They have one in each room of their homes.

Bowl & Candle with Rocks

Supplies

Bowl

Candle (pillar)

Floral clay

Pinecones

Rocks

Place candle in center of bowl. If candle wobbles, stabilize with floral clay. Fill bowl with rocks and add pinecones.

This simple idea is a great way to spruce-up for the holidays or any occasion. Find a bowl you love, or use one you have tucked away in the China cabinet, and add ornaments for a festive look.

Battenburg Lace Christmas Stocking

Supplies

Battenburg Lace

Christmas stocking pattern

Fabric (brocade)

Cut brocade, using Christmas stocking pattern and fabric scissors. Sew stocking, using sewing machine. • Tack Battenburg lace at top, making pleats or gathers as desired, using a sewing needle. Sew around top of stocking. • Turn right side out, fold lace over top of stocking, and iron.

Mosaic Chimney

Supplies

Candle (pillar, tapered, or votive)

Candleholder

Glass chimney

Grout

Mosaic tiles (glass and mirrored)

Super glue

Adhere tiles to glass chimney. Grout tiles, following manufacturer's instructions. Wipe off excess grout, using a damp sponge. Place candle on candleholder. Place chimney over candle.

Mosaic candleholders can be designed in any color range, in any combination of colors, or with any type of mosaic tiles. Try a different combination on each candleholder, and different-shaped candleholders for each person you wish to remember with something special for the holidays.

White Rose Kissing Ball

Supplies

Berry picks

Dried holly leaves

Pinecones (small)

Roses (fresh, white)

Floral foam ball (large)

Wire (18-gauge)

Cut rose stems down to 2". Push rose stems into ball. Cut wire into 4" lengths, using wire cutters. Twist wires around bottom of pinecones, using needle-nose pliers. Push ends of wire into ball. Push picks and leaves into ball as desired. Spray foam ball occasionally to keep moist.

These make a perfect decoration for that special holiday gathering.

Fabric-wrapped Lampshade

Supplies

Fabric (green, organza)

Fabric glue

Lampshade

Wrap fabric around lampshade, turning raw edges inside, beginning at top. Adhere fabric to lampshade where needed to secure.

Multiple lampshades like this can be beautiful when each shade is a different color and they are lined along the mantle.

Floppy Ribbon Wreath

Supplies

Ribbon (lt. green, narrow, fabric; dk. green velvet)

Wire ring

Thread (monofilament)

Cut ribbon into 6" lengths. Finger press in half. • Sew raw edges of pressed ribbon together, using sewing machine. Feed ribbons together through sewing machine for a continuous length three times the circumference of wire ring. • Wrap around ring, securing with monofilament thread. Knot thread to secure. • Tie a loop of velvet fabric to wreath for hanger.

Frosty "Glass" Candleholder

Supplies

Candle (pillar, small)

Frosted glass paint

Glass (tall)

Super glue

Frost glass with glass paint, following manufacturer's instructions. Let dry. Invert glass. Place candle on top of glass.

These candleholders are so easy and inexpensive! Try tying the glass with ribbons or hanging tassels around the neck.

Tile Trivet & Candleholder

Supplies

Ceramic tile

Hot-glue gun and glue sticks

Papier maché fruit (4 apples)

Remove stems from fruit. Adhere fruit to the bottom corners of tile for legs.

Option: Use drawer pulls or glass rocks for legs.

Velvet-wrapped Box

Supplies

Fabric (purple, velvet)

Fabric glue

Fusible web

Papier maché box (tall)

Ribbon (green, wide)

Adhere fabric to box and lid separately with fusible web, following manufacturer's instructions. • Cut ribbon into two appropriate lengths, using fabric scissors, and attach around box sides with fusible web. • Wrap box lid with ribbon, tying ends into bow on top. Fork-cut ribbon tails as shown in Diagram A on page 81. • Adhere ribbon to underside of lid with dab of fabric glue.

Take the time this year to cover several boxes, in different sizes and shapes. They can be reused next year and be just as beautiful.

Decorated Tree

Supplies

Acorn ornaments

Artificial decorations (assorted, jeweled berries; birds; miniature bird's nests, flowers)

Artificial tree (miniature)

Decorative container

Decorative ribbon

Fabric (coordinating, scrap)

Florist foam

Pussy willow branches

Wire (18-gauge)

Fill container with florist foam. Push tree trunk into foam. Wrap fabric around base of tree to cover foam. • Decorate tree as desired with birds, nests, berries, willow branches, and flowers, using wire to secure. • Wrap ribbon around tree for garland.

Gold Cone

Supplies

Beaded trim (gold)

Fabric (purple, velvet)

Hot-glue gun and glue sticks

Papier maché cone

Ribbon (gold, narrow)

Spray paint (gold)

Tassels (1 large gold; 3 small gold)

Paint cone gold. Let dry. • Cut fabric into six triangles, using fabric scissors. With right sides together, sew two triangles together, using sewing machine, leaving one side open for turning. Turn right side out. • Sew trim around two sides of triangle and sew small tassel to each point. • Repeat process to make two more triangles. • Adhere 1" of bottom of triangles to top inside edge of cone, overlapping triangles as needed. • Fold points to outside of cone. Cut ribbon to desired length for hanger. Adhere ends to inside of cone. • Fill cone as desired.

Personalize these cones for the people in your life. The color of paint and the design of the fabric can make each cone you create look very different. For the outdoorsman in your life, make one out of brown corduroy fabric and paint the cone with shades of green and brown. Make one for "Aunt Sarah" out of one of her mothers old hankies and paint the cone ivory.

Gold Star Ornament

Supplies

Leafing adhesive

Leafing sheets (gold)

Papier maché star

Apply gold leafing to star with leafing adhesive, following manufacturer's instructions.

Wire Luminary

Supplies

Candle (pillar or square)

Hardware cloth

Hot-glue gun and
glue sticks

Tin motif (rusty)

Shape hardware cloth into tall, narrow rectangle for luminary. Bend loose ends of hardware cloth over, using needle-nose pliers to secure. Adhere tin motif on center front of luminary. Place luminary over candle. Use caution and keep out of children's reach. Wire becomes hot when candle is lit.

Moss-covered Candleholder

Supplies

Candles (3 tapered)

Candleholder picks

Cold-glue gun and glue sticks

Container (round mouth)

Green moss

Holly sprig pick

Ribbon (2 contrasting colors)

Styrofoam ball (to fit container)

Run a thin line of glue around rim of container and adhere styrofoam ball to container. Apply glue to candleholder picks and push into top of ball. Adhere moss to ball. Tie ribbon into bows and adhere to top center of ball, allowing ends to twist and dangle. Push holly pick in top center of ball. Place candles in candleholders.

Try covering styrofoam balls with unusual materials. Roll them in artificial snow, tiny beads, or cake decorating candies. Use your imagination for a one-of-a-kind candleholder.

Lichen Ball Candleholder

Supplies

Candle (tapered, dripless)

Candleholder (for ball candle)

Candleholder pick

Cold-glue gun and glue sticks

Lichen

Styrofoam ball (to fit
candleholder)

Apply glue to candleholder pick and push into top of ball. Adhere lichen to ball. Place ball on candleholder. Place candle in candleholder pick. Make certain candle is dripless.

These balls can be covered in any type of dried material. They are beautiful made from rosebuds, lavender, potpourri, or try something completely unexpected like beads, yards of ribbon to wrap around the ball, or tiny silk flowers.

Wire Pyramid

Supplies

Berry or leaf sprays (artificial)

Wire (28-gauge)

Wire pyramid

Decorate wire pyramid with sprays as desired. Secure with wire, using needle-nose pliers. Use caution and keep out of children's reach. Wire becomes hot when candle is lit.

Festive "Glass" Shelf

Supplies

Glass (¼" thick, cut to desired dimensions)

Glasses (4, colored, martini)

To determine size of glass to be cut, place inverted glasses desired distance apart. Measure end to end and add 4" for length. Width should be 4" larger than the bottom of the glasses. Set glass on inverted martini glasses.

Miniature Wreath Candle Ring

Supplies (for one ring)

Candle (pillar, small)

Greenery (artificial, wired with berries)

Wire (24-gauge)

Cut greenery long enough to go around bottom of candle, using wire cutters. Bend around bottom of candle and twist ends together to secure, using needle-nose pliers.

For alterantives, try painting wooden rings, braiding ribbons, or tying miniature bows around a metal ring.

Artichoke & Hydrangea Wreath

Supplies

Artichokes (artificial or dried)

Berry sprays

Floral sprays (berry; rose, silk)

Hot-glue gun and glue sticks

Hydrangea (silk)

Lichen balls

Ribbon (gold, narrow)

Wreath (pine with pinecones)

Begin from the center bottom of the wreath and move out, using large items first. • Arrange artichokes, hydrangea, lichen balls, and sprays on wreath as desired. • Adhere items to wreath when desired effect is achieved. • Tie ribbon as desired.

This wreath may be crafted using artificial or live pine, depending on your preference. If made with live pine and fresh flowers, expect it to live 2–3 weeks. Store artificial greenery in a garment bag for use year after year.

Cherubic Table Fountain

Supplies

Bowl (frosted, glass with stand)

Fountain mechanism (small, with light and stand)

Glass rocks (assorted; clear)

Plastic lighting grate

Assemble fountain mechanism following manufacturer's instructions. • Place fountain in bowl. Cut lighting grate to fit inside of bowl to protect fountain mechanism. • Cover grate with rocks. Place bowl on stand.

If your bowl is too dark, the light will not shine through.

Decorated Bottle

Supplies

Bath oil

Decorative bottle cork

Decorative glass bottle

Ornament

Ribbon (ivory, silk)

Fill bottle with bath oil. Close bottle with decorative cork. Hang ornament in center of ribbon. Wrap ribbon around bottle neck and tie ends into square knot.

These make perfect hostess gifts, and can be filled with vinegars, sauces, or whatever is most appropriate.

Decorated Box Lid

Supplies

Ball ornaments (silver, small)

Decorative box (with clasp)

Hot-glue gun and glue sticks

Adhere ornaments in 1" intervals around box lid.

Decorating premade boxes is easy! Personalize by using tiny pieces of jewelry, letters, numbers, beads, whatever you want!

Tasseled Candle

Supplies

Candle (large, pillar)

Candleholder (glass)

Decorative cord (with tassel)

Tie cord around candle. Place candle on candleholder.

Tassels can make a candle seem anything from elegant to natural. They come in everything from beads to jute. Try them all!

Woven Ribbon Frame

Supplies

Craft glue

Frame (flat, wooden)

Ribbons (brown; taupe)

Spray paint (taupe)

Paint frame taupe. Cut six ribbons, each the length and width of frame plus 2", using craft scissors. Lay ribbons on frame, weaving at corners. Adhere ribbon ends to back of frame.

Use ribbons that coordinate, contrast, complement, whatever!

Pear Pitcher

Supplies

Acrylic paints (black; brown; golden brown; med. green; orange; red; white; yellow)

Colored glass pitcher

Glass and tile medium

Paintbrushes (# 6 flat; #12 flat; #01 liner; 10/0 scroller)

Apply glass and tile medium to pitcher, following manufacturer's instructions. Transfer Pears pattern on page 120 to pitcher. • Base-coat leaves med. green; branch brown; and pears golden brown, using #6 flat. • Shade bottom of leaves and one side of vein med. green plus black, using #12 flat. Highlight opposite side med. green plus white. • Shade bottom of branch brown plus black; and top brown plus white. • Wash bottom pear with red to darken. Let dry and repeat. Wash over top pear with orange. Let dry and repeat. • Shade bottom pear where top pear overlaps and along bottom with red. Highlight left side with med. green plus white. • Stroke on fuzzy end of pear with brown plus black, using scroller. • Shade left side of top pear with med. green plus white, using #12 flat. Highlight right side yellow. Shade under leaf with red. • Stroke on tendrils and leaf stems with med. green plus black, using #12 flat. Randomly stroke a wash of yellow and red on leaves to highlight. • Shade pear behind stem with brown and on front of pear with yellow.

Orange & Pear Garland

Supplies

Artificial fruits

Ball ornaments

Garland

Hot-glue gun and glue sticks

Leaf picks

Pinecones

Adhere fruits, ornaments, and pinecones to garland as desired. Randomly adhere leaf picks.

Daisy Bowl

Supplies

Acrylic paints (lt. green; med. green; orange; tangerine; off-white; lt. yellow)

Glass and tile medium

Metal bowl

Paintbrushes (#6 filbert; #0 liner)

Spray sealer (clear)

Apply glass and tile medium to bowl, following manufacturer's instructions. • Sponge orange on bowl. Repeat with tangerine. • Stroke on flower petals with off-white, using #6 filbert. Dot center of flowers with lt. yellow, using tip of paintbrush handle. • Stoke bottom of each flower center with tangerine, using #0 liner. Stroke on leaves with med. green pulled through lt. green, using #6 filbert. • Apply sealer, following manufacturer's instructions.

Red Pepper Bottle

Supplies

Cork

Decorative glass bottle

Decorative stamp

Red chili peppers

Ribbon (½" green)

Sealing wax

Tassel

Fill bottle with peppers and water, then cork. Tie ribbon into bow around neck of bottle. Adhere tassel with sealing wax, using decorative stamp.

Festive Berry Wreath

Supplies

Berry picks

Craft glue

Ribbon (red)

Wreath (styrofoam)

Push picks into wreath and adhere. Continue pushing picks in until entire wreath is covered with berry picks. Let dry. Tie ribbon into bow and adhere to top of wreath.

Christmas is a time of tradition. It is visiting the traditions of the past, creating traditions in the present, and celebrating each tradition in the future. It is the honoring of these traditions that help make Christmas one of the most celebrated seasons of the year.

In today's world, however, time is one of our most precious gifts. So to celebrate old traditions, create new ones, and observe both the old and the new often seems like an impossible task. To help in the celebrating of the old and the creating of the new, *Two-Hour Christmas Crafts* was designed to inspire an unlimited number of ideas.

The ease, the limited cost, and the creativity of each idea on these pages will make this and each new holiday season one that is created and remembered with fondness for a lifetime.

Each page contains four projects that are easily created and fun to give, but they are also only the beginning. Using the general supplies and instructions on pages 107–119, each gift or decorating idea can be redesigned in hundreds of ways. For example, on pages 78–79, the Rock-embellished Cake Plate is such a great idea. The possibilities this idea creates are endless. The decorative edge could be tiny crystal or plastic snowflakes. These are perfect for the nature lover in your life. Or, you may want to take a square, silver serving platter with a smaller square bowl and decorate it with metal silver beads. This is fabulous for complementing an elegant or southwestern decor.

This simple and inexpensive idea could become a family tradition any number of ways. Each year, grown children and their families could take home a different plate and cake to enjoy through the holidays. Or, each year at a family Christmas party, cake plates could be made and filled with Christmas goodies and delivered to a nearby retirement or rest home.

These ideas are a wonderful collection of handmade projects which, when used with your ideas and special touches, are the traditions that symbolize the heart and soul of the season.

General Supplies

The following is a list of materials and tools to have on hand. Additional supplies are listed with individual projects.

Disposable plates

Hand drill and drill bits

Hand saw

Iron and ironing board

Ironing cloth

Masking tape

Nails

Needle-nose pliers

Newspaper

Paintbrushes (general use)

Paper punch (single hole)

Pencil

Sandpaper (fine grit)

Scissors (craft; fabric)

Sewing machine

Sewing needles

Sewing thread

Sponges

Spray bottle (with water)

Stapler and staples

Straightedge ruler

Tin snips

Toothpicks

Transfer paper and transfer tool

Utility knife

Waxed paper

Weighty material (kitty litter, rocks, sand, etc.)

Wire cutters

Beading

The beading projects in *Two-Hour Christmas Crafts* are simple and easy to do. Beads are strung on either a thin beading wire or an 18-gauge wire, or purchased prestrung. They can be twisted and shaped into decorative designs or used as garlands and trims for embellishments.

Beads are available in an endless variety of colors, shapes, and sizes, thus providing unlimited design possibilities. Projects can be customized to individual tastes and desires by merely changing the color of the bead; or, if a smaller or larger piece is desired, simply select a different sized bead and wire.

When selecting beads, make certain to select the appropriate-sized wire. Large-holed beads on a thin wire will be too loose, and obviously, small-holed beads cannot be strung on too thick a wire. Wire is available on spools and in different gauges. The higher gauge numbers indicate a thinner wire, while the lower numbers indicate a thicker wire. The 24- or 30-gauge wire is sufficient for stringing tiny seed and bugle beads, while an 18-gauge wire works well with the larger round and decorative beads. Cut wire lengths longer than necessary to prevent running short. Any excess length can be easily clipped off.

The more commonly used round and oval beads are available in sizes ranging from 3 mm (the smallest) to 25 mm. The tiny round seed beads range in size from 12/0 (the smallest) to 6/0. Bugle beads are elongated seed beads and range in size from 2 mm (the smallest) to 30 mm. Purchase more beads than necessary for completing the project. Beads may crack, roll off the work surface and get lost, or each individual hole may vary just enough that one might not fit the wire. It is better to have more than enough, than to come up short in the midst of the project. Place the beads you are using in shallow dishes or saucers. Plastic paint palette trays are excellent for holding the beads. If working with a small amount of beads, double-sided sticky tape may be placed on the work surface. The tape is helpful in holding the beads in place and preventing them from rolling and scattering about the work surface.

When beading with wire, needles are not necessary as beads easily slip onto the wire. The tools needed for completing the projects in this book are wire cutters (or an old pair of craft scissors) for cutting lengths of wire, and needle-nose pliers for twisting and shaping the wire. All-metal scissors and tweezers also are useful to have on hand. The scissors are good for breaking off chipped or cracked beads without having to unstring all the beads. The tweezers are helpful in picking up and holding small beads.

Box Covering

Ordinary cardboard and papier maché boxes and canisters have been given a rich new look in *Two-Hour Christmas Crafts,* using the simple technique of fabric and paper covering. The wide variety of fabrics and papers in assorted colors, prints, and textures provides unlimited choices for just the right look.

Several different methods have been used to cover the boxes and canisters. The use of fusible web with fabric is the easiest and fastest and works best on simple-shaped boxes. Follow manufacturer's instructions for adhering fusible web to wrong side of fabric. Cut fabric into exact-sized pieces to fit top, bottom, and sides of box. Remove paper backing from web and iron fabric pieces to box parts. Silks and lightweight polyester fabrics are not recommended for use with this method as they may scorch when fusing in place. This method also works well when wrapping a box in a manner similar to wrapping a package.

Wrapping is another relatively simple way in which to cover regular or odd-shaped boxes and canisters. If using paper to cover a box or canister, first cut paper into exact-sized pieces to fit top, bottom, and sides of box. Spray backs of papers with adhesive. Mount papers on box parts.

Place fabric (or paper) wrong-side up on work surface. With canister on its side, center canister over fabric. Snugly wrap fabric around canister and seal seams with fabric (or paper) glue. Add a dab of glue to points and curves on odd-shaped boxes to secure fabric and emphasize the shape. Fold excess fabric to inside of canister and adhere with glue. Again, be aware that certain fabrics, such as silks and lightweight fabrics, may not be appropriate for these types of projects as glues may damage them.

Clayworking

Fun and festive shapes have been designed for *Two-Hour Christmas Crafts*, using brightly colored polymer clay. Two types of polymer clay, air-dry and oven-bake, have been used for these projects. The soft and pliable molding properties of polymer clay allow ease in sculpting and creating designs. Cutting tools, molds, or cookie cutters also may be used to create shapes. Be certain to retire any tools used with polymer clays from food use.

When working with clay, make certain the work surface is clean and smooth as clay easily picks up debris and texture marks. Clay is harmful to wood finishes, so avoid working on a wood surface.

Knead the clay until soft and smooth and the consistency of soft bread dough, then mold as desired. If clay is particularly stiff, it can be softened by adding a purchased kneading medium to the clay or add one drop of baby or mineral oil to each two-ounce block of clay. Allowing a heating pad to indirectly warm the clay also works well. Place the pad under the work surface and warm for five minutes, or place the clay under an incandescent light until warm. Colored clays tend to leave a slight stain on hands. Clean hands between each color use with a dollop of hand lotion to prevent the soiling of colors. (Hand lotion breaks down the oily residue from the clay better than soap.) To attach molded pieces together, press clays tightly together and smooth out the seam. Embellishments, such as beads, buttons, and small trinkets, may be pressed into the clays and baked or air-dried.

Cover baking pan surface with baking parchment paper or 100% rag bond paper. Unless otherwise directed in manufacturer's instructions, bake clay for 20–30 minutes per ¼" thickness at 250°–275°. Turn oven off and allow clay to cool in oven. (Never bake the clay in a microwave oven.) Retire baking pan from food use.

Once the clay has dried or baked and cooled, it can be painted with water-based acrylic paints. If necessary, smooth rough edges with fine-grit sandpaper before painting. Store unused clay in sealed containers in a cool place (such as the refrigerator), away from heat and light.

Decoupaging

Turn plain and ordinary objects into works of art by using the easy technique of decoupage. Anything that can be cut or torn and pasted onto a surface can be used for decoupaging—wrapping paper, magazines, motifs from your favorite greeting cards, fabrics, or natural materials, to name a few. Just as there are many materials to choose from for decoupaging, there are also many surfaces to cover—frames, coasters, boxes, candleholders, and more.

For the decoupage projects in *Two-Hour Christmas Crafts*, decorative papers have been adhered to the project surfaces with decoupage medium. First make certain the surface is clean, dry, and free of any dust particles to ensure the project has a smooth appearance when completed. Apply a coat of decoupage medium to the surface, using a flat paintbrush. Press the papers onto the wet surface, then brush on another coat of medium from the center outward to smooth, protect, and seal edges. Brushing against the edges can lift the papers and result in unwanted ridges. An additional coat or two of decoupage medium will thoroughly seal and protect the surface. Additionally, a varnish sealer may be applied to the surface to permanently seal the surface. If using a heavier-weight paper, apply a coat of medium to the back of the paper as well as on the project surface. This will help the paper adhere to the surface better.

If only one motif is available but a repetitive pattern is desired, simply take the motif to a copy center and have the desired number of color copies made. The motif also may be enlarged or reduced as needed.

Most mediums dry waterproof, but it is recommended that decoupaged projects be hand-washed with a gentle detergent or merely wiped with a clean, damp cloth.

Fabric Embossing with Rubber Stamps

Embossing adds a touch of sophistication to any project. It is the technique of raising the surface of an image. Traditionally, the raised image is created on paper, but *Two-Hour Christmas Crafts* combines the embossing technique with the use of rubber stamps on a napped fabric, such as velvet or velour. The embossed image will produce a beautiful shimmery imprint.

Heat iron on wool setting without steam. Place stamp, rubber side up, on ironing board. Lightly mist right side of fabric, using a spray bottle filled with water. Lay fabric right side down on stamp. Position iron so steam holes do not overlap design. Press iron onto fabric for approximately 20 seconds. Do not move iron. Carefully lift iron and remove fabric from stamp. Repeat process for desired number of imprints.

If added color and shimmer are desired, the stamp can be inked lightly with fabric ink before ironing. However, do not mist fabric with water when using ink.

Fabric Painting

A colorful touch has been added to several of the fabric projects in *Two-Hour Christmas Crafts* with the use of fabric paints. An abundance of paint colors allows you to choose the perfect complementary or contrasting shade to best enhance your project. Fabric paints, in combination with stencils, make creating something special quick and easy.

Acrylic or water-based paints work best with fabric painting because they dry quickly and clean up easily with soap and water. However, the paints must first be mixed with a textile medium. The textile medium prevents the paint from peeling and helps to permanently adhere the paints to the fabric. To use the textile medium, pour a small amount of paint onto a palette. Place a few drops of textile medium on the paint and mix together. The paint will become more transparent as more textile medium is added.

You may wish to try the new fabric paints that have recently been introduced to the craft market. They eliminate the need of having to mix the paints with textile medium, but the color choices are more limited.

Once the pattern is transferred to the fabric, paint background colors first, then paint the details. Fabric painting is like coloring in a coloring book. Be certain to thoroughly clean paintbrushes between each color use.

Allow paint to dry thoroughly. Once dry, heat-set design with a warm iron for 20 seconds on the reverse side of fabric, or use a blow dryer for pre-made fabric projects, such as the lampshade. Clothing with fabric-painted designs may be heat-set in a dryer.

Leafing with Copper, Gold & Silver

Add elegance to a project with the simple addition of leafing. Leafing is available in many colors, though copper, gold, and silver are the most commonly used colors. Gold leafing has been used to enhance several of the projects in *Two-Hour Christmas Crafts*. Leafing may be applied to many surfaces, for almost limitless possibilities.

Leafing is a two-step process. First, following manufacturer's instructions, brush leafing adhesive onto the area in which the leafing will be applied. Allow the adhesive to set until clear or for approximately one hour. Once set, gently pick up leafing with fingertips and press into adhesive. Wipe over leafing with a soft cloth to set it and to remove excess leafing. Keep in mind that leafing crumbles easily. This is normal for producing the desired effect. To protect the finish, apply a coat of clear varnish sealer to the surface. To clean, use a damp cloth.

Experiment with leafing by combining it with other techniques in this book. For example, apply leafing over a painted project. The paint will show through the leafing, giving the project a colorful, sophisticated look. Brush an antique medium over leafing to produce a time-worn appearance.

Mosaicing

If a favorite dish has been chipped or marred, but you just cannot part with it, recycle it into a mosaic project. A gentle tap with a hammer will completely shatter the dish, but all the tiny pieces can then be used to create a beautiful mosaic piece to be enjoyed for years to come. Although mosaic work is an intricate art, the mosaic projects in *Two-Hour Christmas Crafts* are quite basic, simple, and fun to do.

We have covered glass, metal, and plaster objects with mosaics, but most any surface can be covered. Make certain the appropriate adhesive has been selected for your project. A polyvinyl acetate adhesive is excellent for adhering glass and ceramic to wood; silicone sealant for ceramics to glass; epoxy resin for glass to metal; and water-resistant cement-based tile adhesive for ceramics to metal.

Adhere tile pieces to project surfaces with adhesive. Make certain tiles are evenly spaced, and end and corner pieces are evenly cut. For even cuts,

Leafing with Copper, Gold & Silver

or if precise shapes are desired, use tile cutters (mosaic cutters). Allow adhesive to dry thoroughly, following to manufacturer's instructions.

Grout is used to fill the spaces between mosaic tiles. Grouting further secures the tiles and creates a smoother surface. For an exciting touch, color can be added to the dry grout mix, using water-based tempera or acrylic paint. Grout is also available in premixed colors at tile suppliers. Prepare grout, following manufacturer's instructions. Spread grout over tiled surface. A squeegee works well for spreading and ensures a good, even covering. Once all crevices are filled, immediately wipe surface with a damp cloth to remove excess grout from tiles. Allow grout to dry for 24 hours.

Grout sealant is available at tile suppliers. Sealant helps to preserve the color of the grout and protect the grout from staining. Although sealant is not necessary to mosaic projects, it is an option for added protection. Apply grout sealant to grout (not tile) with a flat narrow paintbrush. Let dry.

Painting

Crackle Mediums

To add a weathered appearance to any painted project, simply add crackle medium. The process is easy and the finished product has an aged look without the time it takes for this to happen naturally.

The crackle medium is painted over the base-coated surface—or, the surface may be left in its natural wood state. When dry, a single, smooth coat of paint is brushed over the crackle medium, following manufacturer's instructions. Cracks will appear almost immediately. Different types of crackle medium are available. Some produce small, fine cracks like a broken eggshell, while others create larger, longer cracks that resemble peeling paint. The crackle effect can be adjusted by the amount of crackle medium applied—the more medium, the larger the cracks.

Paintbrushes vs. Spray Paints

Use a paintbrush to paint flat, smooth surfaces. Water-based acrylic paints have been used for most of the projects in this book. The choice of colors is almost endless and clean-up is easy with warm, soapy water. If oil-based paints are used, use turpentine or mineral spirits for cleaning paintbrushes. Avoid soaking paintbrushes in these liquids, as they will weaken the bristles and shorten the life of the paintbrush.

Use spray paints on hard-to-paint items, such as hardware cloth or wire-work. Many types of finishes are available in spray paints, such as matte, pearl, stone, and metallic. Make certain the work area is well covered and protected, and spray in a well-ventilated area. Spray with smooth, even strokes from a distance of about 6"–8" from project surface. Move back and forth across surface, releasing button after each stroke. Overlap strokes. Two thin coats are better than one heavy coat.

Tole Painting

Simple tole-painting techniques, using acrylic paints, can add color and charm to projects. Once the basics are mastered, more complex techniques and designs can be completed. Understanding the following terms and techniques will be useful in completing the tole-painting projects in *Two-Hour Christmas Crafts*:

Base-coat: Apply several smooth coats of paint. Allow paint to dry, then sand lightly with a piece of brown paper bag between coats. It is better to apply two or three thin coats of paint instead of one thick coat.

Double-load: Load one side of the paintbrush with one color of paint and the other side with another color. Stroke paintbrush on palette to blend where the two colors meet. Paint project.

Dot: Dip a toothpick or the tip of a paintbrush handle into paint and tap on project to make a round dot. Dip each time for uniform dots, or tap several times to make decreasing-sized dots.

Floated Color: This is done to achieve all shades and highlights of a color. Wet a flat paintbrush and touch to a paper towel until the shine from the water disappears. Dip one side of the paintbrush into the paint and stroke on the palette to soften the color. The paint should be the darkest on the side dipped in paint and fade to clear water on the other side.

Fly Speck: Dip stencil paintbrush or old toothbrush into paint that has been thinned to an inky consistency. Hold the loaded paintbrush approximately 6" above project and pull your finger across the bristles.

Load Paintbrush: Stroke paintbrush back and forth through paint so paintbrush has color on both sides of bristles but is not dripping with paint.

Stipple: Load old, scruffy, flat paintbrush in paint. "Pounce" paintbrush up and down on palette to remove excess paint. Pounce paintbrush on project.

Paintbrushes

The use of the correct paintbrush is important to achieve the desired effect. All tole-painting projects in *Two-Hour Christmas Crafts* specify which paintbrush is used for each step. However, projects not requiring tole-painting techniques, such as Snowman Clay Pin on pages 20–21, do not name specific paintbrushes. The following is a brief description of tole-painting paintbrushes and their uses. They may be used in other projects where applicable.

Flat Paintbrushes: Flat paintbrushes are used for base-coating, shading, and highlighting. Their sizes are even-numbered, beginning at #2. The higher the number, the wider the paintbrush. Choose the size, depending upon the size of the area to be painted.

Round Paintbrushes: Round paintbrushes are used for delicate lines and detail work. Their sizes are odd-numbered, beginning at #1. Again, the larger numbers indicate a larger paintbrush.

Scrollers: Scrollers are used for very fine line work and scrolls. Their sizes range from 18/0 (the smallest) up to 3. Using a scroller is similar to working with an ink pen. Load the scroller with paint that is the consistency of ink. Stroke the scroller on the palette to remove excess paint from tip. If tip is overloaded, the desired effect will not be achieved.

Sewing (Needlework)

Sewing projects in *Two-Hour Christmas Crafts* have been created by using either elegant fabrics from the fabric store or by using a favorite old garment, curtain, table linen, etc. Projects made from these old favorites add a special, sentimental meaning.

Consider the weight, pattern, and color when selecting fabric for a particular project. A dainty, pink floral chintz may not be appropriate for a gift intended for a man. On the other hand, a blue-striped denim cloth would be perfect for a masculine pillow.

Additionally, select a fabric that is appropriate for the use of the project. A project that may be laundered frequently should not be made from a non-washable fabric. Prewash fabric to test for shrinkage and colorfastness. Oftentimes, fusible web can be used in place of sewing, if desired.

Fraying can be prevented by trimming seam allowance, using pinking shears or dabbing raw edges with a liquid fray preventative.

Cross-stitching also has been applied, using the pattern on the fabric as the square grid. To cross-stitch, simply sew "X's" in each square grid, making certain the top cross-stitch is going in the same direction.

The projects have been completed using simple sewing stitches that can be sewn either by hand or machine. When making Christmas stockings, please follow the instructions of your favorite Christmas stocking pattern for assembly. For other sewn projects, the following terms are provided:

Baste: Basting is a long, loose stitch used to hold an item together until it is permanently sewn.

Tack: Tacking is a method whereby a few stitches are repeatedly hand-stitched over each other to secure items together.

Gather: Gathering employs the basting stitch and the thread is then pulled to gather the fabric together.

Hem: Hemming is completed by pressing the raw edge under ¼", then turning it under another ¼" and stitching to secure.

Stenciling

With the wide variety of stencils available—from florals, to alphabets, to handmades—a personal and sentimental touch can be added to any project. An ordinary piece of fabric and a plain silver container have been stenciled in *Two-Hour Christmas Crafts* to give the pieces that oh-so-special effect.

For handmade stencils, transfer the pattern onto a piece of clear acetate or a piece of lightweight cardboard. Use a craft knife or a single-edged razor to cut out the portion of the design to be stenciled from the acetate or cardboard. Be certain to work on a protected surface. A piece of glass works great, or use a cutting board.

Secure stencil to project with masking tape, or spray back of stencil with stencil adhesive and let dry. Position stencil on project and press to secure stencil. Load stencil brush with acrylic or water-based paint. Blot off excess paint on paper towel. If too much paint is left on the brush, it will seep underneath the stencil. Bounce the stencil brush up and down across the open portion of the stencil. Clean the brush with soap and water. Let brush dry thoroughly before loading with another paint color. It is important for the brush to be completely dry. For faster drying, use a blow dryer.

An alternative to using the stencil brush is to purchase a package of make-up sponges. They are inexpensive, easy to use, and the extra sponges are handy for multiple-color use. Once the design is completely stenciled, gently remove the stencil. If paint is still damp, wipe stencil with a clean cloth. If paint has dried, clean stencil with rubbing alcohol.

When stenciling on textured fabric, such as velvet, additional coats of paint need to be applied for complete coverage. Let paint dry between each coat. Do not remove stencil until desired look has been achieved.

Wireworking

Take an ordinary piece of wire and twist and shape it into an appealing design or heartfelt phrase. Attach the wire design to a candle, a frame, or any number of projects to create a unique gift.

Wire is available in different thicknesses called gauges. The gauges are numbered. The smaller the number (i.e. 18) the thicker the wire. A larger gauge number (i.e. 30) indicates a thinner wire. Wire is most often sold on spools, but precut lengths are also available. The standard color of wire are silver, however gold and copper copper are readily available. New, vibrant colors, such as pink, metallic red, and blue, are also beginning to appear on the market.

Thin wires are easy to twist and shape with your hands and can be cut with metal scissors. To form words or shapes, first write the word or create the design on a piece of paper for use as a pattern, then shape the wire, following the pattern. For simple twists, wrap the wire around a pencil, then slide the pencil out. For larger twists and swirls, wrap the wire around a bottle. Any shape can be used as a form.

Thick wires require wire cutters for cutting and needle-nose pliers for shaping. Hold one end of wire firmly in hand. Bend and shape opposite end of wire as desired, using needle-nose pliers. Crimp the wire, using needle-nose pliers, to hold shape or to hold lettering in place.

In addition to forming simple shapes, wires also have been soldered together for several of the projects in *Two-Hour Christmas Crafts*. Lead-free soldering wire and a soldering iron are needed for these projects; as well as flux, which is available at hardware stores. Flux is an acid that attracts the soldering wire and adheres the wire to the metal to be soldered. Use caution when soldering. Make certain the work area is covered, or solder over a concrete floor. Do not allow flux or solder to touch skin or other surfaces. Apply a drop of flux on the area to be soldered. Unroll approximately 4"–5" of soldering wire, keeping hold of spool. Heat tip of soldering wire with iron. Wire will melt. Drip melted wire on area treated with flux. Attach wire to soldered area. Let harden.

Patterns

Rose Corner

Pears

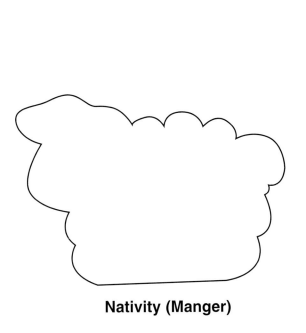

Nativity (Manger)

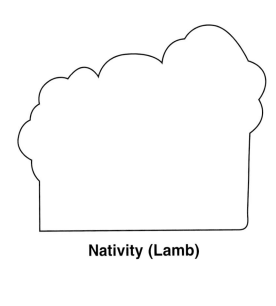

Nativity (Lamb)

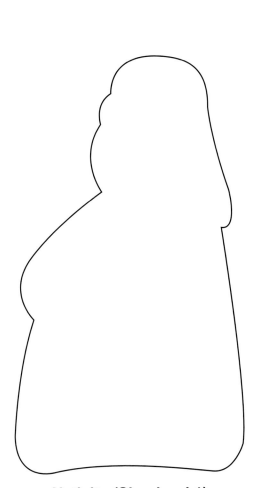

Nativity (Shepherd 1)

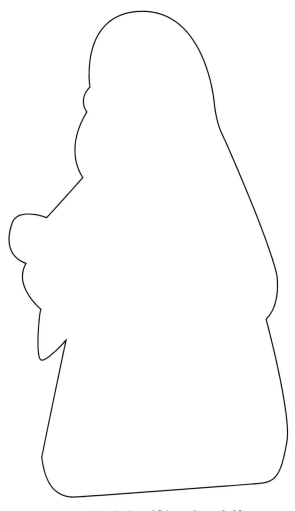

Nativity (Shepherd 2)

121

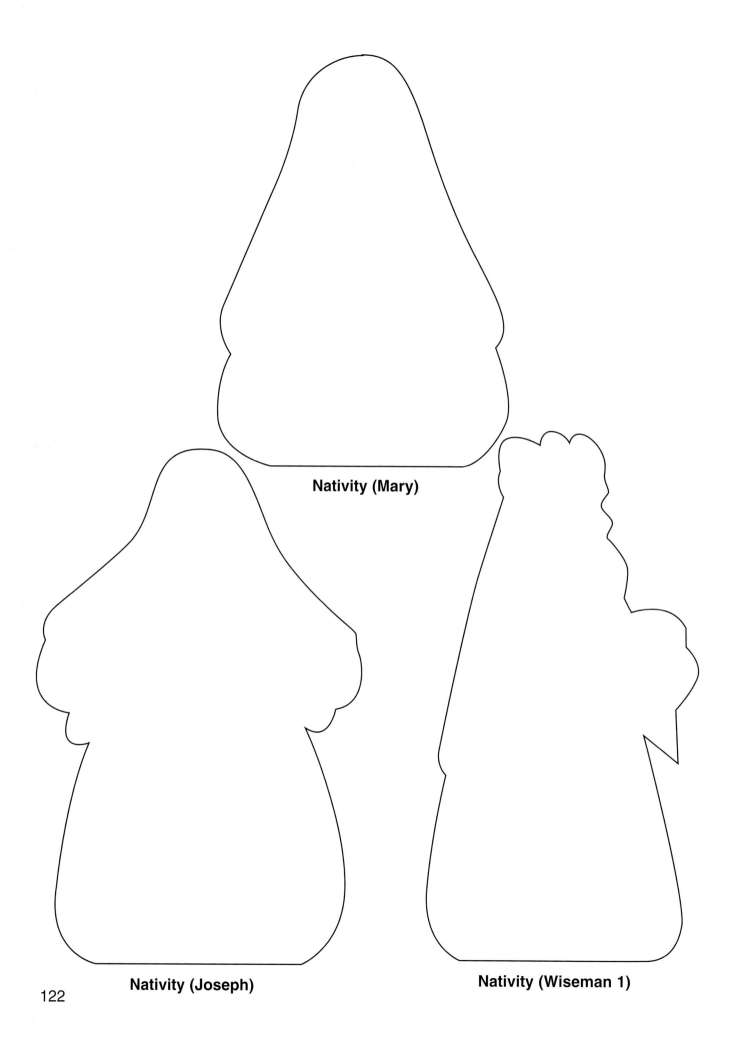

Nativity (Mary)

Nativity (Joseph)

Nativity (Wiseman 1)

122

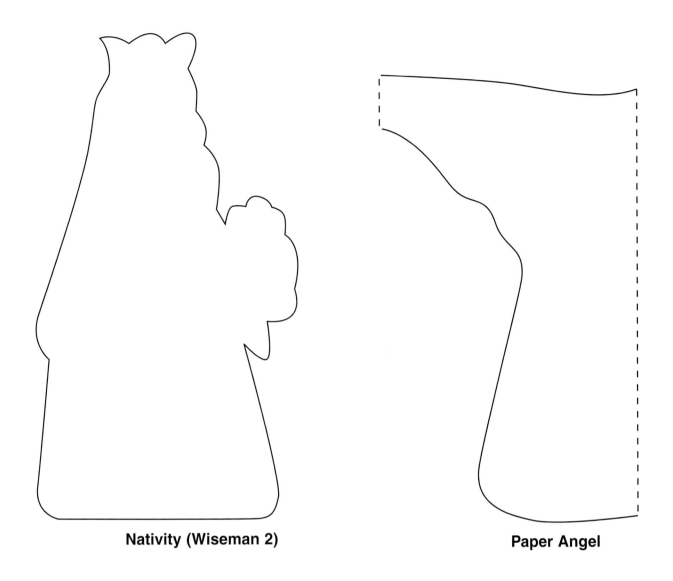

Nativity (Wiseman 2)

Paper Angel

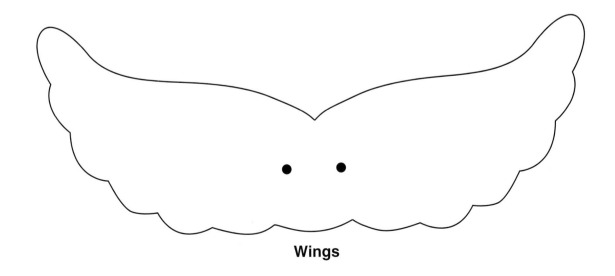

Wings

Pine Spray—enlarge 20%

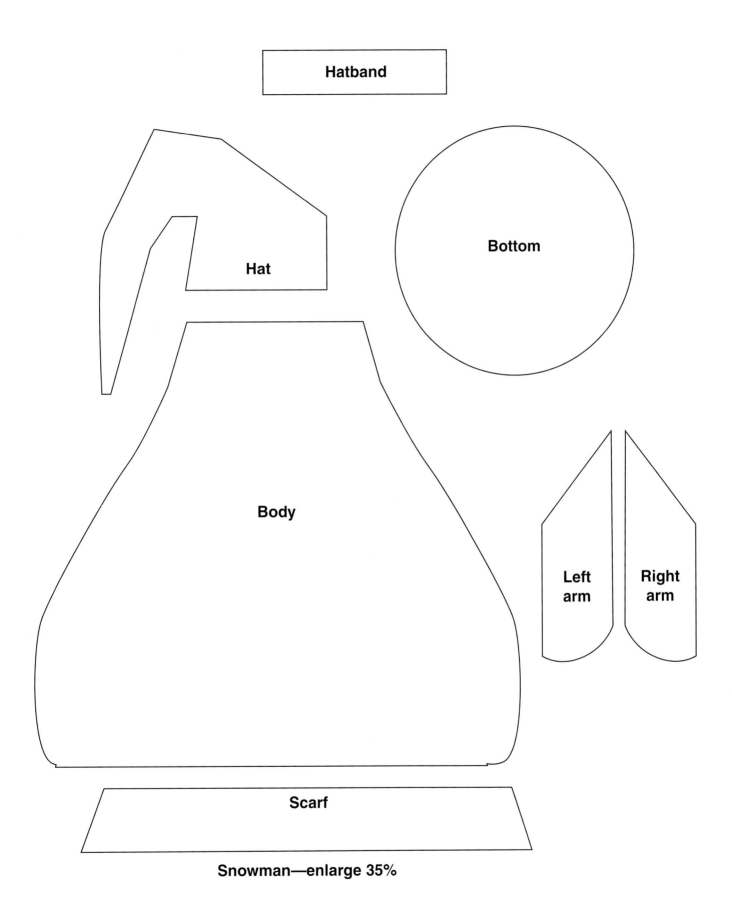

Hatband

Hat

Bottom

Body

Left arm

Right arm

Scarf

Snowman—enlarge 35%

Holly

Snowman Scene

About the Author

Michele Thompson credits her mother for her creativity. "She taught me the meaning of the saying, 'Necessity is the mother of invention.'" As a child, Michele learned from her mother's example how to decorate and make beautiful things on a budget. She professionally decorates homes and businesses, specializing in Christmas decorating. Michele lives in Heber, Utah, with her husband Troy and her four children Spencer, James, Creighton and, Chloe.

Acknowledgment

Thank-you to Holly H., Areta, Pauline, Amber, Holly F., Becky, Jo, Barbara, Ann, Jamie, Kevin, Dana, and Kass. I appreciate the time and talents you shared.

Metric Equivalency Chart

cm—Centimetres
Inches to Centimetres

inches	cm	inches	cm	inches	cm	inches	cm
⅛	0.3	5	12.7	21	53.3	38	96.5
¼	0.6	6	15.2	22	55.9	39	99.1
½	1.3	7	17.8	23	58.4	40	101.6
⅝	1.6	8	20.3	24	61.0	41	104.1
¾	1.9	9	22.9	25	63.5	42	106.7
⅞	2.2	10	25.4	26	66.0	43	109.2
1	2.5	11	27.9	27	68.6	44	111.8
1¼	3.2	12	30.5	28	71.1	45	114.3
1½	3.8	13	33.0	29	73.7	46	116.8
1¾	4.4	14	35.6	30	76.2	47	119.4
2	5.1	15	38.1	31	78.7	48	121.9
2½	6.4	16	40.6	33	83.8	49	124.5
3	7.6	17	43.2	34	86.4	50	127.0
3½	8.9	18	45.7	35	88.9		
4	10.2	19	48.3	36	91.4		
4½	11.4	20	50.8	37	94.0		

Index